Easy Activities for Building Social Skills

by Nancy Jolson Leber

SCHOLASTIC
PROFESSIONAL**B**OOKS

New York • Toronto • London • Auckland • Sydney • Mexico City • New Delhi • Hong Kong • Buenos Aires

To my daughters Holli and Abby,
of whom I am so very proud . . .
each and every day.

Acknowledgments

Special thanks to Dr. Myrna Shure, professor at MCP Hahnemann
University in Philadelphia, for her input, insights, and expertise
with problem-solving techniques and her generosity with her
time; Dr. Lois Berman; Ilene Rosen; Marcia Kessler and Barbara
Wolf-Dorlester of the Churchill School, New York City; Sharon
DellaRose of the Norbel School and Ann Burman of Beth Tefiloh
Nursery School, both in Baltimore, Maryland.

"Five Little People" by Judy Lalli. From *I Like Being Me* by Judy Lalli, M.S.,
copyright © 1997 by Judy Lalli. Used with permission of Free Spirit Publishing
Inc., Minneapolis, MN, www.freespirit.com. All rights reserved.

Cover design by Josué Castilleja

Cover photographs by Sean Justice (Image Bank), Ellen Senisi (The Image Works),
Ariel Skelleg (The Stock Market), David Young-Wolff (PhotoEdit)

Interior design by Ellen Matlach Hassell
for Boultinghouse & Boultinghouse, Inc.

Interior illustrations by Shelley Dieterichs

Interior photographs courtesy of *Early Childhood Today*

ISBN: 0-439-16353-6

Contents

Introduction

We live in a society where the difference between right and wrong is often blurred. Parents may hesitate to set limits for their children; teachers may face challenges in managing their classes. Supporting social development through classroom routines each and every day can help lessen these issues.

Research has shown that there is a high correlation between social and academic behavior, and that the level of social competence in preschoolers is a good predictor of their academic success in elementary school. Children with strong social skills experience fewer adjustment problems both as students and as adults. Since some studies indicate that problem behavior in preschoolers is likely to continue through adolescence, it would seem that prekindergarten and kindergarten are the perfect places to begin to teach social skills. At this age, young children are experiencing the most rapid mental growth and can be encouraged to develop behaviors and attitudes that will enhance positive interactions with peers.

Learning interpersonal skills and conflict resolution at an early age is important in helping prevent more serious problems later on. Children begin to relate the way they think with how they feel—and how they feel influences their actions. The average 4-year-old, for example, can learn to accept differences. He or she can learn that people have feelings, that behaviors have causes, and that problems have many solutions. As a result of this knowledge and understanding, children may become more caring and cooperative.

By advancing the social development of young children in school, we can help empower them not only to make and maintain friendships but also to incorporate behaviors that will be of lifelong benefit to them—and to our society.

How to Use This Book

This book presents 19 essential social skills lessons to help young children develop a greater understanding of themselves and their classmates. The skills included in *Easy Activities for Building Social Skills* are just a starting point. You'll weave the ideas into your day and all you do! Also keep in mind that you'll need to eliminate, revise, or adapt activities to suit three- and four-year-olds.

Skills are taught and reinforced through:

- direct teaching
- role-play
- poems and stories
- discussion
- puppet play
- visual aids
- hands-on activities
- games
- songs

You may want to spend a day, week, or month on one skill, depending on the needs and maturity of your group. Each of the 19 lessons follows a similar format and is accompanied by a reproducible page to spark discussion or to reinforce a skill. Elements of each lesson include background information, an introduction to the skill, suggestions for helping children respond, and an extension activity for follow up. Suggestions are also provided for finding moments in your daily routine to reinforce the skill or to extend the skill by reading related age-appropriate book(s).

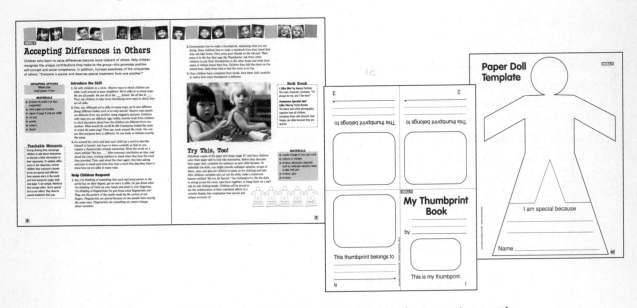

The most important ingredient in using this book, however, is you, the teacher! Children thrive on the encouragement and validation that comes from your attention to their efforts.

Accepting Differences in Others

Children who learn to value differences become more tolerant of others.
Help children recognize the unique contributions they make to the group—
and develop awareness of the uniqueness of others: "Everyone is special and
deserves special treatment from one another!"

GROUPING OPTIONS
Whole class
Small groups of four

MATERIALS
- pictures of people (cut from magazines)
- chart paper and markers
- copies of page 46 (1 per child)
- ink pad
- pencils
- scissors
- stapler

Teachable Moments
During sharing time, encourage children to talk about themselves. Mention to children how everyone's thumbprints are special and different from anyone else's in the world and how everyone's paper dolls (see page 7) are unique. Reinforce this concept often: *You're special but so are others. They deserve special treatment from you.*

Introduce the Skill

1. Sit with children in a circle. Observe ways children are alike: *Look around at your neighbors. We're alike in so many ways. We are all people. We are all at the ___ School. We all live in ___.* Then ask children to take turns identifying more ways they are all alike.

2. Next, say: *Although we're alike in many ways, we're also different. Being different makes each of us very special.* Use magazine pictures to discuss ways people are different from one another. Continue with ways you are different (age, hobby, favorite food) from children to foster discussion about how the children are different from one another. *What would the world be like if everyone looked the same or acted the same way?* Then say: *Look around the circle. You can see that everyone here is different. No one looks or behaves exactly the same.*

3. Go around the circle and ask each child to say a word to describe himself or herself. Ask children to listen carefully so that no one repeats a characteristic already mentioned. Write the words on a chart titled "We Are . . ." After everyone contributes an idea, read aloud the chart, inviting children to stand when they hear the word they provided. Then read aloud the chart again, this time asking everyone to stand each time they hear a word that describes them to show how they are alike in many ways.

Help Children Respond

1. Say: *I'm thinking of something that each and every person in the world has on his or her fingers, yet no one's is alike. Do you know what I'm thinking of?* Hold up your hands and point to your fingertips. *I'm thinking of fingerprints! Do you know what fingerprints are? They are the pattern of the marks made by the surface of our fingers. Fingerprints are special because no two people have exactly the same ones. Fingerprints are something we cannot change about ourselves.*

2. Show children how to make a thumbprint, talking about what you are doing as you are doing it. Then show children how to make a mini-book from their sheet that they can take home: *First, press your thumb on the ink pad. Then press it in the box that says My Thumbprint.* Ask three other children to put their thumbprints in the other boxes and write their name or initials below their box. Children then fold the sheet on the dotted lines. Help them fold so that the cover is on top.

3. Have children look carefully at their completed books to notice how every thumbprint is different.

Book Break

I Like Me! by Nancy Carlson (Penguin, 1990)
The main character concludes, "I'll always be me, and I like that!"

Someone Special Just Like You by Tricia Brown (Scholastic, 1984)
The black and white photography captures how all children, including those with physical challenges, are alike because they are special.

Try This, Too!

Distribute copies of the paper doll shape (page 47) and have children color their paper doll to look like themselves. You might provide wallpaper samples, scraps of fabric, yarn, and glue for children to paste on for clothing and hair. After they decorate their paper doll, complete the sentence as each child dictates. Help children cut out the dolls, then make a classroom banner titled "We Are All Special." Use clothespins to clip the dolls to string across the room, tape them together, or hang them on a wall side by side linking hands. Children will be proud to see the collaboration of their individual efforts in a colorful display that emphasizes how special and unique everyone is!

MATERIALS

- copies of page 47 (1 per child)
- crayons or markers
- decorative materials such as wallpaper samples, fabric scraps, and yarn (optional)
- glue (optional)
- scissors

Recognizing Strengths

All children have strengths. As teachers, our role is to reinforce the strengths they have while building new ones. Give children experiences in which they can be successful. Let them know that trying hard is a great strength!

GROUPING OPTIONS

Whole group
Small groups
Individuals

MATERIALS

- poster board and marker
- copies of page 48 (1 per child)
- scissors
- pencils
- paper
- crayons
- hole puncher
- yarn

Teachable Moments

To validate children's strengths, when you see them doing something well, point it out. Remind children how everyone is good at some things and not as good at others. But with practice, they can improve.

Introduce the Skill

1. Sit with children in a circle and play a guessing game. Say: *I'm thinking of someone who is a big help when it's time to clean up. Yesterday he washed all the paintbrushes. Who am I thinking of?* Continue in this manner until you have mentioned each and every child. Then explain that everyone has strengths, or things he or she does well. Go around the circle and have volunteers provide a strength they have or see in others.

2. Next, brainstorm a list of different things that children can do well. For example, some may have strengths in sports, such as kickball, soccer, or gymnastics. Others might excel in singing or playing an instrument, painting or drawing, or dancing. Some children might speak two languages. Others may be good at reading or at math. Still others might be helpful to classmates or skillful at making new friends. Record this list on a poster titled "I Can . . ."

> **I Can . . .**
> dance
> paint
> draw
> sing
> kick the ball
> catch a ball
> read
> speak Spanish
>   and English

3. Count up the number of things on the list and talk about how all these strengths will help the class during the year in so many ways.

Help Children Respond

1. Distribute copies of the activity master on page 48. After children cut out the badges, help them to complete the badges with what they think they do well. Provide help with spelling or have children dictate to you what they want written on their badges. For example: *I'm a soccer player* or *I'm a reader.* Have them write their name on the line.

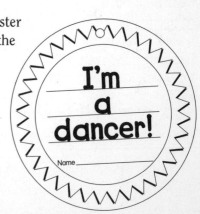

> **I'm a dancer!**
> Name

2. When children have completed their badges, punch a hole at the top and hang it on a piece of yarn. Knot the ends so children can wear their badges as necklaces. Allow a few minutes for children to examine each other's badges.

Try This, Too!

1. Invite a volunteer to pretend that he or she is someone else in the classroom. Have the volunteer act out something the other child is good at. Invite children to guess the identity of the child being portrayed.

2. Read aloud a short biography, such as *The Many Lives of Benjamin Franklin*, by Aliki. Ask children to talk about what they think were Franklin's strengths, for instance, *He was a great inventor*. Explain that Franklin was a very great man because his inventions helped so many people. Ask children how Franklin made our world a better place.

3. Have children name a favorite storybook or cartoon character. Together, brainstorm a list of what that character does well. Then discuss ways his or her strengths helped solve problems in the story.

MATERIALS

■ biography of a familiar person, such as *The Many Lives of Benjamin Franklin* by Aliki

Book Break

Cosmo Zooms
by Arthur Howard
(Harcourt Brace, 1999)
Every dog on Pumpkin Road is really good at something except Cosmo, until he accidentally discovers a skateboard.

Recognizing Nonverbal Language

Children who are able to "read" nonverbal clues may have an easier time making friends. One way to learn about how someone is feeling is by talking to that person. Another way is by watching someone's actions. Help children understand that even the smallest movements of the body can send messages and communicate important information.

GROUPING OPTIONS
Whole class
Small groups

MATERIALS
- plastic hand mirror
- chart paper
- markers

Teachable Moments

As situations occur in the classroom, help children recognize nonverbal communication by interpreting their body language with a comment such as, "You have such a big smile on your face, Kate. Can you share what's making you so happy?" Try to notice and comment on children's efforts at "reading others."

Introduce the Skill

1. Ask children to close their eyes and count to three. Briefly leave the room and re-enter, skipping and swinging your arms with a big smile on your face. Ask children how they think you are feeling. Say: *There's a word to describe how I am feeling—happy. How could you tell how I was feeling?* Elicit that the look on your face, the way you moved, and the position of your body showed that you were feeling happy.

2. Next, look sad by frowning and lowering your head. Ask children how they think you are feeling now and how they can tell.

3. Invite children to take turns looking happy or sad. Provide a hand mirror and encourage each child to view himself or herself. Ask others in the group how each child is feeling, and ask them how they can tell. Talk together about the ways people's faces often show what they are feeling.

4. Use your face—and the rest of your body—to show that you are excited, then scared. For example, jump up and down to show excitement; take a cautious step backward to show fear. Ask children to describe the actions that show your feelings. Then demonstrate other actions that have special meanings: put your hands on your hips; shake your head; clap your hands. Have children tell you what they think each action means.

5. Make a poster with children to tell how people are feeling: *Look at the face. Look at the body.*

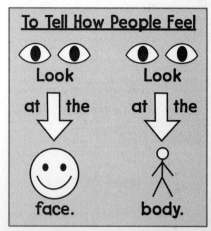

To Tell How People Feel

Look at the face.
Look at the body.

Help Children Respond

1. Remind children of the two ways to observe how people are feeling: *Look at the face. Look at the body.* Explain that they can show their own feelings, as well as understand the feelings of others, by using their face and their body. Have children stand in their places as you ask them to show you how they would feel if—
   - They're playing a game and lose a turn.
   - They get a favorite toy for a birthday.
   - They don't feel well and have to miss a friend's party.

2. Point out that when we understand what makes other people feel the way they do, we understand them better. Have children take turns acting out feelings such as happy, sad, excited, scared, angry. Explain that they can use their face and their body, but they cannot use any words. Next, invite volunteers to show how they might respond to each child's feelings.

Try This, Too!

Distribute back-to-back copies of the mini-book (pages 49 and 50). Help children cut, fold, and staple. Next, ask children to write their name. Read aloud each sentence in the mini-book. For each picture, ask why the child might be feeling that way. Brainstorm possible reasons, for example: *On page 2, Ling might be angry because she can't go outside to play, the cover of her new book got dirty, her brother borrowed her favorite ball and now can't find it. On page 3, Maria might be happy because she is going to the movies with her friend, her mom goes on a trip and brings her a gift, her dog has puppies. On page 4, Matt might be surprised when he hits his first baseball, gets a tricycle for his birthday, or sees and hears the loud noise of fireworks for the very first time.* Repeat this for the pictures of the children on mini-book pages 5–8. Then invite children to color the pictures.

MATERIALS

- copies of pages 49 and 50 (1 per child)
- pencils
- crayons
- scissors
- stapler

Recognizing the Feelings of Others

A young child's ability to predict and interpret others' feelings is one of the keys to making friends. Young children also need to recognize their own feelings and how their actions affect how other children feel and respond to them.

GROUPING OPTIONS
Small groups

MATERIALS

■ *How Are You Peeling? Foods With Moods* by Saxton Freymann and Joost Elffers (Scholastic, 1999)
■ copies of page 51 (1 per child)
■ ball
■ toy truck
■ chart paper
■ crayons and marker

Teachable Moments

Young children may grab items from classmates without thinking about another person's feelings. Encourage them to think before acting, by asking, for example: *If you grab Margo's lunch bag, then how might she feel? What else could you do?* Support children's appropriate responses and their efforts to treat classmates with kindness and respect.

Introduce the Skill

1. Sit with children in a circle and read aloud *How Are You Peeling? Foods With Moods*. Use the clever photographs to discuss different feelings. Ask children if they have ever felt the emotions shown.

2. Next, say: *Today we're going to play a game called "If/Then." I'll start a sentence and you finish it. Here we go.* As you read each sentence, replace the names below with names of children in the group. Encourage children to think about the way they would feel in each instance. Then go around the circle, soliciting responses:
   • *If Lana loses her new baseball cap, then she might feel ___.* (sad)
   • *If Brian's friend gives him a gift, then he might feel ___.* (happy)
   • *If someone bumps into Lee on his bike, then he might feel ___.* (angry)
   • *If Lupe's parents plan a party for her birthday and don't tell her about it, then she might be ___.* (surprised)

3. Create other "If/Then" sentences that relate specifically to the class. Then have children make up sentences of their own that tell how they feel in a particular situation. After each one, ask: *Do you think you might feel that way, too, [name of another child]?* Point out that although we are different people, many of our feelings are the same.

Help Children Respond

1. Distribute copies of page 51. Say: *Let's look at this picture and think about how the children might feel. Let's call the girl with the basketball Grace. We'll call the boy holding the truck Harry.* Start a discussion about the picture by asking:
   • *What is happening in this picture?* (Possible answer: Grace has the ball, but Harry seems to want it.)
   • *If Harry grabs the ball, how might Grace feel?* (Possible answer: sad or angry)
   • *What else might Harry do to get the ball?* (Possible answers: He might ask politely for the ball; he might suggest that they play catch.)

Use this format to model questions and answers: If students suggest behavior that is inappropriate or aggressive, gently guide them to think of more appropriate approaches that might yield both harmony and positive results.

2. Continue the "If/Then" game with children and ask:
   - *If Harry asks for the ball and Grace says yes, then Harry might feel ___.*
   - *If Grace says no, then Harry might feel ___.*
   - *If Grace says, "You can have the ball if you give me your truck," then Harry might say ___ or ___.*
   - *If Harry says yes, then Grace might feel ___.*
   - *If Harry says no, then Grace might feel ___.*
   - *What is something different that Grace could do or say so that both she and Harry feel good?* (Possible answer: Grace could suggest that they play together.)

2. Using a ball and truck, or similar props, ask volunteers to act out scenes about playtime. After each one, reinforce appropriate behaviors supporting children's efforts.

3. Invite children to color the picture on page 51. Record their resolutions to Grace and Harry's problem at the bottom of each child's page.

Try This, Too!

Invite volunteers from an older class to act out short scenes about when classmates made them feel happy, angry, or sad. Ask them to use their face and their body to show how they are feeling. If a sad or angry feeling is portrayed, encourage discussion about how the situation could have worked out better.

----- **Book Break** -----

Today I Feel Silly and Other Moods That Make My Day **by Jamie Lee Curtis** (HarperCollins, 1998) Rhyming language and fanciful art contribute to the upbeat mood of the book that concludes, "Whatever I'm feeling is OK."

Sometimes I Feel Like a Storm Cloud **by Lezlie Evans** (Mondo Publishing, 1999) Bright art and similes are used to describe a child's feelings.

Sometimes I Feel Like a Mouse **by Jeanne Modesitt** (Scholastic, 1996) Through animal-related similes and art, children recognize that everyone has many feelings, and all feelings are okay.

Listening

Good listening is critical for success in school. A good listener is better able to follow directions, participate in discussions, and ask meaningful questions. Good listeners tend to be aware of what's around them and pay particular attention to people and their feelings.

GROUPING OPTIONS
Whole group
Small groups or pairs

MATERIALS
- chart paper or poster board
- marker or chalk
- magazines

Teachable Moments
Ask children to observe how others listen when they are speaking during class discussions or sharing time. Remind children to follow the rules on the Good Listeners poster. Encourage good listening with a pat on the back or smile.

Introduce the Skill

1. Sit in a circle with children to play a listening game. Say: *I'm going to the moon and I'm taking [a cat].* Have the person next to you repeat what you said and add another item. Continue around the circle. Ask children what strategies someone needs to do well at this game. (listening, remembering, rehearsing)

2. Invite a volunteer to describe (and demonstrate) how to play a simple game, such as Go Fish. As the volunteer explains, play with your shoelaces and pretend to not listen. When he or she has finished the explanation, ask the group: *Now what do you think will happen when [child's name] and I start to play the game?* Call on children to suggest what might happen.

3. Ask why it is important to listen. Discuss with children the things we can do to be good listeners, such as:
   - Stop what you are doing.
   - Be quiet.
   - Look at the speaker's eyes.
   - Concentrate. Ignore other things around you.
   - Think about what you hear in order to understand.
   - Ask questions if you don't understand.
   - Repeat what you heard to yourself.

   List the main ideas on a chart and read them aloud.

Help Children Respond

1. Invite a volunteer to be the "teacher." Ask him or her to think of a favorite game and to explain two rules to the group. Then tell the other children that [child's name] will be the teacher and you will be a listener for the next few minutes. As the "teacher" speaks, doodle with a pencil. Then have the "teacher" repeat the instructions. Put your pencil down as you maintain eye contact, then follow the directions.

2. Discuss with children how you behaved like a careful listener. With the group, determine which steps you followed from the poster. (Keep in mind that social rules regarding eye contact vary across cultures.)

3. Working in pairs, ask children to teach classroom rules or a game to each other. As they take turns playing "teacher," walk around, noticing and commenting on the behaviors you see.

Try This, Too!

1. Invite a volunteer to stand and briefly tell about his or her weekend or something he or she has done recently. When the speaker is finished, summarize what was said by saying, *So you are saying that . . .* or by asking a question, such as *So since you didn't like the movie you saw this weekend, what movie have you seen lately that you liked?*

2. Mention that making a comment or asking a question about what a speaker has said shows that you are an interested listener. It also shows that you want to make sure you understand what is being said. Then encourage children to make their own comments about what was said.

3. Distribute copies of page 52. Read aloud the sentence starter and model how you might complete it. Then have children work in pairs. Give out topics or have children choose their own to talk about with their partners. Walk around and offer feedback about each child's listening skills.

4. At the end of each discussion, ask children what they learned about their partner. Say: *[Child's name], when you stopped, looked, and listened, what did you learn?* Record each child's answer on his or her page.

5. Provide crayons for children to color the elephant. Then collect all the pages to make a class book. Punch holes at the top and bind the pages together using colorful yarn. Create a cover for the book. Title it "Good Listeners."

MATERIALS
- copies of page 52 (1 per child)
- crayons
- scissors
- yarn or stapler

Book Break

How to Be a Friend: A Guide to Making Friends and Keeping Them by Laurie Krasny Brown and Marc Brown
(Little, Brown, 1998)
The ups and downs of friendship are described in real-life situations. Includes practical tips on listening and paying attention to what friends say.

Good Listeners

Greeting

A greeting is a child's first immediate contact with another person, and can easily set the tone for the rest of the interaction. Some children may greet you with enthusiasm. Others may be shy, unable to make or maintain eye contact with you. Help children understand that a warm and friendly greeting is a great way to let others know you like them. (Keep in mind that different cultures view greeting styles differently.)

GROUPING OPTIONS
Whole group
Pairs

MATERIALS
- chart paper or poster board
- marker
- paper lunch bags
- paper fasteners
- crayons
- red construction paper
- scissors

Teachable Moments

As you visit different places in school, encourage children to practice greeting others. Model great greetings as children enter the classroom each day. Discuss with children how your greeting made them feel. Then discuss how they greeted you and how that made you feel.

Introduce the Skill

1. Have children sit in a circle. Tell them to listen carefully and watch what you do next. Go around the circle and smile and greet each child by name, maintaining eye contact with each one. Vary your greetings and even add a wave.

2. Ask children what they noticed about how you greeted them. Help elicit that you smiled, said "hi" or "hello," used their names, and looked at the eyes of the person you were greeting. Write these steps on a poster titled "Glad to Meet You!"

Glad to Meet You!
1. Smile. ☺
2. Say "hi" or wave. ✋
3. Look at the person. 👁 👁

3. Divide children into pairs to greet each other. Then you might want to repeat the "Glad to Meet You!" steps. Say: *This is what you can do when you see someone you know or walk by someone you recognize. Greet that person by smiling, saying hello and using that person's name if you know it, and looking at him or her while you do this.* Point to each step on the poster as you say it.

Help Children Respond

1. Prepare two paper bag puppets for this activity. Attach a red construction paper smile with a paper fastener to each bag. Draw big eyes and the rest of the face, using markers or crayons. Then tell children that you brought along two friends. Introduce the two puppets, displaying one at a time. Say: *You're going to watch while ___ and ___ meet and greet each other. Look carefully and tell me if you think they're greeting each other in a friendly way.* First, position the puppets' mouths into frowns and tilt their heads away to avoid eye contact as you move them toward each other. Ask: *What do you think they could do to be friendlier?* Remind children how you greeted everyone in the group. Elicit that you smiled, said

"hi," used their names, and looked at the eyes of the person you were greeting. Use the puppets to demonstrate this behavior.

2. Now have children play a game called "Let's Fix This Greeting." Invite a volunteer to place a puppet on one hand, while you work the other puppet. Ask the rest of the group to watch the puppets meet. Then greet your helper's puppet, eliminating one of the steps on the poster. Ask children to identify which part of the greeting was forgotten. Reenact the greeting, including every step.

3. Put one puppet on each hand and have children line up to greet each puppet before returning to their tables. Remind them of the steps on the poster.

4. Have children make their own paper bag puppets. Have them cut mouths from red construction paper and color the paper bags. Help them attach mouths using the fasteners. (You may want to prepunch a hole for the fastener in each bag.) Children can write their names on the back of the puppets before using them for the next activity. (You might later add the puppets to the dramatic play center.)

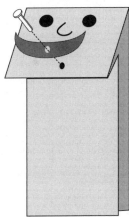

Book Break

Oops! Excuse Me Please! and Other Mannerly Tales
by Bob McGrath
(Barrons, 1998)

Say the Magic Word, Please
by Anna Ross
(Random House, 1990)

Both books present appropriate greetings in child-oriented situations.

Try This, Too!

1. Have partners take turns greeting each other's puppet, using the steps on the poster. Encourage them to choose different ways to greet the other puppet and then share those greetings with the class.

2. Distribute copies of the mini-book on page 53. Help children fold and tape their books as shown below. Next, ask children to write their name on the line. Read aloud each sentence in the mini-book. As you read, ask children to use their puppets to reenact the steps for a friendly greeting.

3. Let children color the pictures in their mini-books. They can share their books at home.

MATERIALS

- copies of page 53 (1 per child)
- tape
- crayons

Using Polite Words

We show respect for others by using words like *please, may I,* and *thank you* when asking for and receiving help. Let children know that when they speak respectfully, others are more likely to respond in a positive way.

GROUPING OPTIONS
Whole group
Small group

MATERIALS
- copies of page 54 (1 for whole group activity; 1 per pair for small group activity)
- chalkboard and chalk
- scissors
- bag
- number cube
- game markers

Teachable Moments
Display the words *please* and *thank you* on cards in the classroom as gentle reminders for children to use polite words. Remark on polite behavior.

Introduce the Skill

1. When children are seated quietly, ask them to watch you and to listen carefully. Ask a child to hand you something nearby. Say: *May I please have the ___?* After the child has done so, say, *Thank you.* Repeat with other children.

2. Ask what polite words you used when asking for an item. *(May I please . . .)* Explain that we use the word *please* when we want help. We use the words *may I* when we ask for permission to do or take something. Ask what polite words you used after the item was given to you. *(Thank you)* Explain that we use the words *thank you* when someone does something nice for us. Point out that the words *please* and *thank you* are among the most important words people use. Continue by saying that it is polite after someone thanks you to say, *You're welcome.*

3. Discuss with children that we say the word *please* when we want help because it is polite. Ask how they would feel if you had said, "Give me the ___!" instead of "May I please have the ___?" Point out that when people use the word *please*, it makes you want to respond or help them. When we use the words *may I* to ask for permission to do or take something, we wait until permission is given before we do the activity or take the object.

4. Have children brainstorm some situations when it is polite to use the phrases *excuse me* and *I'm sorry.*

Help Children Respond

1. Write the words *please* and *thank you* on the chalkboard. As you point to each, read it aloud. Review when we use the words by asking: *What word do we use when we want help?* Reinforce positive responses by pointing to the word *please*. Ask: *What words do we use when someone does something nice for us?* Point to the words *thank you*.

2. Next, play the "Please and Thank You" game as a whole-group activity. Cut the pictures from the game board on page 54 and place them in a bag. Have children take turns choosing a picture from the bag and describe the situation pictured. Then do some acting with the child. For example, a child selects a picture showing someone

who wants to borrow a marker and says, "May I borrow your marker please?" Point out the word *please* on the chalkboard. Continue the acting by holding out a marker so the child may respond by saying, "Thank you." Say, "You're welcome" in return. Point out appropriate behavior.

3. Once children are familiar with the situations, distribute copies of the game board on page 54. Have children work in pairs to play the "Please and Thank You" game. Provide plastic chips for children to use and one number cube to roll. Children may take copies home to play.

Book Break

Manners by Aliki
(Greenwillow, 1990)
Children learn a variety of manners in this book that uses a comic strip format.

Say the Magic Word, Please by Anna Ross
(Random House, 1990)
Sesame Street characters use polite words in child-oriented situations.

I Have a Cold by Grace Maccarone
(Scholastic, 1999)
Children will recognize polite talk related to a boy's bout with a cold.

Try This, Too!

Play Mother, May I? with children. Ask them to stand beside each other in a line on the opposite side of the room from you. Call on a child to move in a certain way, for example: *Juan, you may take one scissor step* or *Akasha, you may take three baby steps.* After each direction, children must ask permission, using the polite words (*May I . . .*). When you respond *Yes you may*, they say *thank you* before actually moving. Respond by saying, *You're welcome.* Without the appropriate polite response, children cannot move from their spot. Continue until most children have reached your side of the room.

Asking Questions

Young children need to know that it's great to ask questions—they're a good way to gather information. Some children who understand a lesson or conversation don't ask questions. Other children may not ask questions because they are hesitant to reveal their confusion. Help children understand that whether they are afraid, confused, or just curious, asking questions can help them. Asking questions is the first step to learning more!

GROUPING OPTIONS
Whole group
Pairs

MATERIALS
- copies of page 55 (1 per child)
- bag
- 10 index cards
- 2 plush male and female puppets (optional)
- chart paper
- marker

Teachable Moments

During discussions, sharing time, or reading time, acknowledge children who ask good questions. When needed, restate or rephrase their questions to model how to construct effective questions. Be sensitive to children who have a more difficult time forming questions.

Introduce the Skill

1. Say: *Imagine that it is your first day at school. I hand you a note and say, "Please take this to Mr. Lopez." What might happen if you don't ask any questions?* Point out that the note might not get to the right person or the child might get lost in the building. Brainstorm with children some questions they could ask to obtain more information. For example, *Who is Mr. Lopez? Where would I find him? How do I get there?*

2. Discuss reasons why we ask questions. Explain: *We ask questions to get permission to do or take something. We ask questions to try to find out more information. Asking questions can help us understand what is being said, or what we need to do. We also ask questions to learn about things we don't know. We feel less worried if we find out about things that are new to us.* Present this situation: *If you learned you were going to be staying with a new baby-sitter, you might feel upset. What questions might you ask your family?* Point out to children that if they asked questions to find out who the baby-sitter is and what she likes to play or do, they might feel more comfortable. Asking questions also lets the people we talk to know that we are interested in what they are saying.

3. Mention that it is important to ask questions in a nice way. When a question is asked politely, it is more likely that the answer will be helpful. Mention that often, in the classroom, children are asked to raise their hand to ask a question.

4. To practice asking questions, write each of the following on an index card. Place the cards in a bag and have each child choose one. Read the card aloud. Have the child think of an appropriate question to ask if he or she were the person in that situation. Model the first one:
   - You want to invite a friend to come to your house.
   - You're not sure how to complete the worksheet from your teacher.
   - You can't find the school nurse's office.

- You want help in cleaning up the spilled juice.
- You don't know where the paintbrushes are.
- You want to help your teacher by erasing the chalkboard.
- Tomorrow is your birthday and you want to bring cake to school.
- You need help tying your shoelaces.
- A new girl is in your class and you don't know her name.
- You are on the playground and your friend falls down.

Invite others to give feedback. Discuss and evaluate the questions children asked.

Help Children Respond

1. Distribute copies of the activity master on page 55. Ask children to look at the pictures. Encourage them to think about the kinds of questions the children in the pictures might ask. Talk about question words, including *who, what, where, when, why,* and *how.* For each picture ask: *What does the child need to ask? Who should the child ask? When should he or she ask? What is a nice way to ask?*

2. Use two puppets to role-play each scenario. Invite a volunteer to work one puppet, while you work the other one. Encourage students to use their question words at the beginning of their questions. When necessary, restate children's questions by rephrasing them. Have children repeat any questions you model for them.

3. Have children color the pictures. Invite pairs to act out each situation or one that is similar.

Try This, Too!

Play Ten Questions with children. Tell them you are thinking of someone in the room. They must identify that person by asking up to ten questions. Go around the room and let each child ask a question. Begin by modeling appropriate questions. Children can also play this game in small groups.

Book Break

The Best Teacher in the World **by Bernice Chardiet and Grace Maccarone** (Scholastic, 1996)
The real-life experience of getting lost but being afraid to ask questions will hit home with children as they read about a little girl who tries to deliver a note for her teacher.

Using the Telephone

Answering the telephone—and even making calls—is something most young children are likely to have done. Help children understand that courteous talk will enable them to better communicate with others. Remind them of the polite words they have already learned and used: *please* and *thank you*!

GROUPING OPTIONS
Whole group
Pairs

MATERIALS
- 2 or more toy or real telephones
- copies of page 56 (1 per child)
- crayons
- scissors
- craft sticks
- paste or tape

Teachable Moments
Add play telephones and a message pad to the dramatic play center. Remind children to use polite words when they speak on the telephone.

Introduce the Skill

1. Before introducing the skill to children, cut out the figures of the bunny and the bear from the reproducible sheet on page 56. Then use them to act out the scripts below. Ask children to listen carefully to both conversations as you read the scripts.

A. *(ding-a-ling)*
Hello.
Hello. This is ___.
May I please speak to ___?
Just a moment please.

B. *(ding-a-ling)*
What do you want?
Go get ___.
Wait. (Slam down receiver.)

Discuss with children which conversation was more polite and why. Help them identify polite words, such as *hello, may I,* and *please.* Point out that it is polite for callers to identify themselves.

2. Tell children to imagine they are holding a telephone, or have volunteers use the puppets you have made. Repeat the first conversation above, reading the words in italics and asking children to provide the appropriate responses chorally. Do this as a group a few times, saying the responses with children until they can respond on their own.

3. Continue with the following scripts, first modeling polite conversations as above and then having volunteers to take one puppet and act out one side of the conversation.

C. *(ding-a-ling)*
Hello.
Hello. Is Pat there?
May I tell him who is calling?
This is Alex.
Just a minute, Alex.

D. *(ding-a-ling)*
Hello.
Hello. May I please speak to Lee?
I'm sorry. You have the wrong number. *
I'm sorry I bothered you. Good-bye.
Good-bye.

E. *(ding-a-ling)*
Hello.
Hello. This is Brett.
May I please speak to ___?
This is ___.

*Caution children not to provide their name or phone number to a caller. It is preferable to ask what number the caller wants.

4. Ask for volunteers to pretend with you. After each conversation, have other children listen and talk about what they saw and heard. Help them identify all the polite words that were used.

   F. *(ding-a-ling)*
   Hello.
   Hello. This is Ms. Lane. May I please speak to your mom?
   I'm sorry. My mom can't come to the phone.
      May I take a message?
   Yes, please ask her to call me tomorrow.
   Okay, Ms. Lane. Good-bye.
   Good-bye.

Help Children Respond

Distribute copies of page 56 and have children color their puppets. Help them cut out their puppets along the dotted lines and paste or tape craft sticks onto the back. Have each child write his or her name on the back of each puppet, then use them to role-play polite telephone conversations. After each role play, talk about polite behaviors. Pairs of children can use puppets to have other pretend telephone conversations.

----- **Book Break** -----
Manners by Aliki
(Greenwillow, 1990)
Children learn about appropriate telephone conversation in this book that uses a comic strip format.

Oops! Excuse Me Please! and Other Mannerly Tales
by Bob McGrath
(Barrons, 1998)
McGrath presents appropriate telephone talk in child-oriented situations.

Try These Ideas, Too!

- Set up a listening center, tape-recording the conversations already practiced in this lesson and leaving adequate time for children to respond where there words appear in italics. (You may want to have another voice record an appropriate response for children to listen to so that they can check their work.)

- Bring in old telephones for children to play and practice with.

Encouraging

Compliments make people feel good. They show that you've noticed something positive about another person or something special he or she has done. Encouragement shows empathy and understanding of something that may be difficult for someone else to do. Help children understand appropriate and polite ways to compliment and encourage those around them.

GROUPING OPTIONS
Whole group
Pairs

MATERIALS
- brown construction paper or craft paper
- scissors
- tape
- copies of page 57 (1 per child for each meeting)
- colored copier paper (optional)

⌐Teachable Moments⌐
Encourage children to give compliments or encouraging comments. Notice their efforts when you hear them by filling out a leaf from the reproducible sheet with the compliment. Ask the child who offered it to hang it on the classroom Compliment Tree. When the tree is full, have a celebration.

Introduce the Skill

1. In advance, create a tree trunk with branches from brown construction paper and hang it on the wall. Then print copies of the activity master on page 57 on colored paper. (Completed leaves will be taped onto the branches.)

2. Invite children to sit in a circle. Go around the circle, giving a well-deserved compliment to each child. For example, say: *I like how hard you worked on your block building, Marissa* or *You are waiting so patiently, James.* Then say: *I gave each and every one of you a compliment. How did it make you feel? Why?*

3. Discuss what a compliment is. Ask several children how they felt when they received your compliment. Explain that we feel good about ourselves when we are complimented. Mention that you felt good about yourself when you gave each compliment because you were recognizing how hard everyone was working and how kind and helpful they were being. Point out that you noticed, for example, how Marissa smiled when you complimented her, James said "Thanks" when you complimented him, and other positive reactions or behaviors you observed.

Help Children Respond

1. Discuss with children how they might compliment classmates. Brainstorm a list, based on what they believe is important.

2. Mention that sometimes a compliment may not be appropriate. For instance, at soccer practice, we may try to kick the ball but might miss it or not kick it well. It is inappropriate to give a compliment such as, "You kicked the ball really well." Instead, this is a time to offer encouragement by saying something such as, "You're trying very hard" or "Keep your eye on the ball while you kick and you'll get it!" Friends encourage friends.

Try This, Too!

1. Ask children to give another child a compliment sometime during the day and remember what it was. They can share it at closing circle time.

2. Distribute copies of the activity master on page 57. Record the compliments on leaves children have cut and attach them to the Compliment Tree. When the branches are full or at the end of each week, have children take their leaves home.

3. As an independent activity, suggest that children give a compliment or encouragement to someone at home that evening and share the compliment and any response to it with the class the next day. Call this sharing time "Compliment Show-and-Tell."

MATERIALS

■ copies of page 57 (1 per child for each meeting)
■ pencils
■ scissors
■ tape

Book Break

Ronald Morgan Goes to Bat **by Patricia Reilly Giff**
(Penguin, 1990)
A boy with little skill but lots of spirit encourages his teammates on the school baseball team.

***Feelings* by Aliki**
(Greenwillow, 1984)
This Reading Rainbow selection talks about compliments.

Joining In

Children use a variety of ways to join the play of their peers.
Some linger close to a group before asking to join in, others
jump right in. Encourage children to think of what they can
do or say to indicate that they wish to join in.

GROUPING OPTIONS
Whole group
Small groups

MATERIALS
- blocks or toy
- chart paper
- marker
- crayons
- copies of page 58 (1 per child)
- scissors
- paste

Teachable Moments

Provide positive feedback to
children who follow appropriate
strategies to successfully join
existing groups and activities.
Compliment group members who
consider the feelings of those who
wish to join their activity.

Introduce the Skill

1. Have two or three children play with blocks or a game while the others sit in a circle around the group. Tell children that you are going to be a student in the classroom. Say: ___, ___, and ___ are *playing a game. I want to play with them. What do you think I could do?* Let children contribute their ideas.

2. Explain that you are going to show two different ways to join the group. Discuss the outcomes of each. First, while the group is playing with the game, stay on the opposite side of the room. Then barge in and sit right down. As they play, pretend to not know the rules. After a brief period, ask those observing: *How might the players feel about my joining them? What do you think might happen? What might they say? What might they do?* Next, have the group resume playing as you watch them. At a logical break in play, politely say, "I'd like to play, too" or "That looks like fun. Can I play?"

3. Review the steps you followed the second time by asking: *If I want to join a group activity, should I stand nearby or far away?* Point out that sometimes when you are close to an activity, the group may see you and invite you to join in. *If I want to join an activity, is it better to join in the second I feel like playing or watch for a good time? Why? If I want to join an activity, is it better to ask nicely or just plop myself down and tell everyone I'm playing? How might this make people feel? If I ask to join an activity, is it better to ask very quietly and shyly or use a brave, clear voice? Why?*

4. Have children brainstorm ways they might ask to join an activity. Discuss each idea with the group.

5. Summarize how to join an activity. Write the steps on a chart like the one at left for later reference.

Join In

Stand near. 👤👤👤

Look. 👁👁

Ask. 🙂❓

Help Children Respond

1. Distribute copies of page 58, one per child, and read aloud the title, "I Want to Play." Show children how to fold the stand-up book along the dotted lines.

2. Discuss with children the two pictures in each column and help them decide which shows the better way to join an activity. For example, reiterate that you should 1) stand nearby rather than far away from a group you wish to join to let others know you are interested; 2) wait, watch, and ask questions rather than simply jump in; and, 3) be part of a group rather than take it over. Have them draw an X on each picture showing the less effective way to join in, then color each remaining picture. Finally, ask children to cut along the solid cutting lines and paste them in their picture-frame boxes. Help children write their name on back of their stand-up books.

Book Break

Horace and Morris But Mostly Dolores by James Howe
(Atheneum, 1999)
Three friends are always together until Horace and Morris join a boys' club and Dolores is left out.

Feeling Left Out by Kate Petty
(Barrons, 1991)
A new boy in the neighborhood feels left out until he recognizes how he can enjoy new friends in different ways.

How to Be a Friend: A Guide to Making Friends and Keeping Them by Laurie Krasny Brown and Marc Brown
(Little, Brown, 1998)
Joining in is one issue examined by the dinosaur characters in this invaluable guide that explores the ups and downs of friendship.

Try This, Too!

Divide the class into small groups to practice how to act and what words to use when joining an activity. Give each group a board game or suggest games, such as Bingo or a beanbag toss. Have children in each group take turns walking away from the group and then trying joining in. Nearby, display the poster with the steps to "Join In." Offer suggestions and reminders to children encountering difficulty. Support the positive actions of children who join, as well as the group members who respond appropriately.

MATERIALS
■ board games, Bingo, or beanbags

Waiting Your Turn

Learning to be patient is an important social skill for youngsters to master. Children need to learn that they cannot always be first and must take turns with classmates and peers. Those who develop this skill at an early age tend to have an easier time with classmates.

GROUPING OPTIONS
Whole group
Small groups

MATERIALS
- copies of page 59 (1 per child)
- crayons

Introduce the Skill

1. Have children sit in a circle. Say: *Let's say you have a question for me but you see that I am talking to someone else. Can I talk to you and to someone else at the same time? What can you think of to do while you wait?* Accept each of their suggestions and add additional ideas, including the following: *Wait quietly. Do something else. Ask someone else. Say "Excuse me" if you must interrupt, especially for an emergency.*

2. Help two volunteers imagine that one of them is a teacher who is helping the other one, a student. Explain that you will be another student. Pretend to be thinking out loud but talk to the observers in the group: *I need help. Ms./Mr. ["teacher"] is talking to ___. I need to wait. They might be talking for a little while. So I think I'll color in the meantime. Hmm. How do I let Ms./Mr. ___ know I need help? What should I say?* Elicit a response from the group. Once you've gotten the appropriate response, continue and say: *Excuse me, Ms./Mr. ___. I need help when you're free.* Finally, pretend to color and wait your turn.

3. Reiterate that someone may not be able to help two people at the same time. Ask questions such as: *Did I expect the teacher to help while she was busy? Did I wait there and maybe make Ms./Mr. ___ uncomfortable? Did I disturb the teacher every few seconds?* Have a volunteer recap the appropriate steps to take while waiting your turn.

4. Acknowledge that it can be hard to wait. Ask children to give examples of when they have had to wait for their turn, for instance, when playing a game, when waiting for a snack to be distributed, or when a parent was talking on the phone. Together, brainstorm a list of constructive things to do while waiting for one's turn. When appropriate, say, "Good thinking," to let children know that they are good problem solvers.

Teachable Moments

When children do something productive while waiting for your help, let them know you noticed. If waiting is a particular problem in the classroom, reinforce the behavior of children who are positive models by making a weekly chart or daily list of the names of children who have been patient.

Help Children Respond

1. Tell children you are going to play a game called "What Would You Do?" First, distribute copies of page 59 and discuss what is going on in each picture:
   - A child is near the end of a long line at an art display.
   - A child hurt her finger on the playground.
   - A child doesn't understand what to do in a workbook and the teacher is helping someone else.
   - A child wants to see a pet bunny but others are crowded around the cage.
   - A child feels sick and his teacher is talking to another adult.
   - A child is eager to show her teacher the picture she painted but the teacher is helping other children clean their brushes.

2. Divide the class into small groups, one for each picture. Ask each group to decide on what they would do in their situation. Then call on each group to act out their scene, showing what they would do if they were the people in the picture. When necessary, ask children, "Can you think of something different to do while you wait?" and have them act it out again.

3. Invite children to color the pictures.

Try This, Too!

Play a game in which children need to wait. Try a board game such as Candy Land or play a game of T-ball outside. If children do not wait to take their turns, you might say, "I know it's hard to wait," and encourage them to think of something different to do while they wait. You may need to ask questions that focus on feelings, such as: *How do you think [child's name] feels when you take a second turn before he or she has had a turn?*

> ### Book Break
>
> ***It's Hard to Share My Teacher*
> by Joan Singleton Prestine**
> (Fearon, 1994)
> When a boy has to wait for his teacher's help, he assists his classmates and realizes the importance of sharing when there are many children and only one teacher.

MATERIALS
- board game (optional)

Taking Turns/Sharing

Taking turns and sharing help children learn to cooperate. One way to develop cooperative behavior is through games. Another is to encourage the sharing of classroom tools and playthings. The goal is to create a sense of community that promotes generosity and concern for others through sharing!

GROUPING OPTIONS
Whole group
Pairs

MATERIALS
- crayons and coloring books, or a handheld video or other game
- copies of page 60 (1 per pair of children)
- scissors
- construction paper
- crayons
- paste

┌ Teachable Moments ┐
Many activities throughout the school day, including the listening center, block area, and use of art materials, involve taking turns and sharing. Plan cooperative games and activities such as cooking that encourage children to use these skills.

Introduce the Skill

1. Act out a situation with a child in which both of you have coloring books, but you are hoarding the crayons. Or you could be playing a handheld video game and not give the child a turn. After a minute, whisper to the child to ask for a turn. When the child asks for a turn, be reluctant to share and use a whining or complaining tone. Ask children who are watching how they feel about your actions.

2. Discuss with the child some ways you can both get a turn. Then reenact the roleplay. Ask children how this was different from the first one. Elicit that you shared and took turns by thinking of ideas and speaking politely. Point out that you cooperated.

3. Talk with children about cooperation. Ask: *What makes a game or job fun to do with someone else?* Explain that cooperation often involves sharing. Continue: *Let's say you and I are playing a video game. What is an example of sharing when playing a video game?* Point out that taking turns is an example of sharing. Next, ask: *Would it be fun for both of us if I used the game the whole time? How could we take turns?* Then review by saying: *Yes, you could go first and I would wait. That's how we'd take turns. That would make playing the game a lot more fun for both of us!* Finally, ask children for different ways to cooperate. Encourage children to try their ideas the next time they play together.

4. Summarize by saying: *When we work or play together, we need to cooperate by taking turns and sharing. When we take turns and share, we get along better with others. Everyone has a chance to play and to use the materials.*

Help Children Respond

1. For each pair of children, distribute one copy of page 60, one pair of scissors, one piece of construction paper, and several crayons. Also distribute one jar of paste to be shared by two pairs. Explain that partners will decide together how to color, cut, and put together the puzzle before pasting it onto construction paper. As children work

together to complete this project, walk around the room and notice and make mention of cooperative behavior.

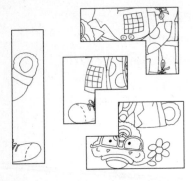

2. Invite partners to display their completed puzzles. Ask: *Did you cooperate by sharing and taking turns? How did it work out? What did your partner do when you wanted a certain color crayon? How did you decide who would use the scissors?*

3. Have children summarize how they feel when someone doesn't share with them, as well as how they feel when someone takes turns.

Try This, Too!

To encourage cooperative play, suggest a game of Caterpillar. Pairs of children lie on the floor on their stomachs. One child holds onto the ankles of his or her partner to make a two-person caterpillar. They then move together, slithering across the floor to connect to another pair to make a four-person caterpillar, then an eight-person caterpillar, and so on. You may want to direct when each pair connects to another pair in order to avoid confusion and to reinforce the skill of waiting (Skill 12).

Book Break

The Doorbell Rang
by Pat Hutchins
(HarperCollins, 1986)
More and more friends arrive to share a plate of cookies.

Oops! Excuse Me Please! and Other Mannerly Tales
by Bob McGrath
(Barrons, 1998)
One of these tales deals with taking turns.

Being a Good Sport

We often encourage children to be good sports, but learning to play fair is a big step that requires turn-taking, listening, cooperation, and playing by the rules. When playing with others, children must wait their turn, share, practice patience, and encounter a certain amount of disappointment.

GROUPING OPTIONS
Whole group
Pairs
Small groups

MATERIALS
- chalkboard and chalk
- 2 hand puppets with arms that will allow puppeteers to write with chalk on the board
- number cube
- chart paper and marker (optional)
- copies of page 61
- crayons

⌐Teachable Moments⌐
Provide opportunities to play cooperative games in the classroom and on the playground, and include cooperative activities in the curriculum. Discussion after these activities and games will help to ensure that positive behaviors transfer to other classroom situations. Encourage children to review the chart of their ideas on how to play fairly.

Introduce the Skill

1. Ask children to sit in a circle. Draw a Tic-Tac-Toe grid on the chalkboard. Have a volunteer tell the rules for playing Tic-Tac-Toe. (One player is X; the other is O. Players take turns marking a box with X or O. The first one to get three Xs or Os in a row across, down, or diagonally calls out, "Tic-Tac-Toe!" He or she is the winner.)

2. Next, introduce two hand puppets and tell children that the puppets are going to play Tic-Tac-Toe. Ask them to listen to the puppets to decide if they are being good sports. Explain that being a good sport means following the rules of the game and winning or losing politely. Use the following example:

   PUPPET 1: *Let's play Tic-Tac-Toe.*
   PUPPET 2: *Okay. I'll be X.*
   PUPPET 1: *No, I'll be X.*
   PUPPET 2: *Forget it. Then I'm not playing.*
   PUPPET 1: *Okay. I'll be O, but then I go first.*
   PUPPET 2: *No, X always goes first.*
   PUPPET 1: *It doesn't have to. Ready?*
   PUPPET 2 (complaining): *If you go first, I'm not playing.*
   PUPPET 1: *Then don't play. Charmaine, do you want . . .*
   PUPPET 2: *Fine, go ahead.*

Have each puppet use chalk to put Os and Xs on the chalkboard grid in the sequence shown. Have the puppets "talk" as they play. For example, "Now I'll put an X in this box" or "Hmm, where should I put my O?" With step 7, continue the script.

₂ X		₃ O
₅ O	₁ O	₇ O
₄ X	₆ X	

   PUPPET 1: *Tic-Tac-Toe! I have three in a row.*
   PUPPET 2: *That's not fair. You cheated!* (Puppet erases the O just written in.) *You put your O where I was going to put my X next.*
   PUPPET 1: *I didn't cheat. You're cheating!*
   PUPPET 2 (whining): *I don't want to play with you again!*

3. After the puppet play, ask children if the puppets thought about each other's feelings. Have children recall what happened, why the game turned out poorly, and what could be improved. Mention to children that when they play a game, they should act the way they want to be treated.

4. Brainstorm ways to be a good sport. You might write children's ideas on a chart. Point out that being a good sport helps everyone to have fun.

Help Children Respond

1. Have pairs of children play Tic-Tac-Toe on the chalkboard or with paper and pencil. After they finish, ask them to share how they decided who would be X and O, and who would go first.

2. Distribute copies of page 61 or copy it onto a chart so you can point as you read. Read the finger play to children as they follow along. Reread until they can join in with you, at least for the repetitive phrases. Have children identify the ideas in the poem that they might think about when they play.

3. Then have children do a choral reading. Divide the class into five groups, assigning each group a line. Everyone can say the lines together, except for the words in quotes, which the assigned group says. Children can use a crayon to underline the words they will say. Another alternative is to have everyone say the lines together and five volunteers, each with a puppet (such as the puppet made for Skill Lesson 6), say aloud their part that appears in quotation marks. Repeat with different volunteers so that everyone gets a chance.

Book Break

Oops! Excuse Me Please! and Other Mannerly Tales by Bob McGrath (Barrons, 1998)
One tale deals with a good sport who loses a race but knows to say "Congratulations" to her opponent.

Ronald Morgan Goes to Bat by Patricia Reilly Giff (Penguin, 1990)
An inexperienced baseball player is big on team spirit.

Try This, Too!

Introduce cooperative games in the classroom or reinvent familiar games to foster inclusion and group problem solving. For example, play a modified version of Musical Chairs. Rather than encouraging pushing and eliminating a player each time the music stops and another chair is removed, tell children that all the players must fit into fewer chairs. Teamwork is required as children squeeze onto the remaining chairs and consider other alternatives to exclusion, such as sitting on laps.

MATERIALS

■ cassette player and music

Helping Others

Children are likely to feel proud and good about themselves when they do something to help others. They like to show how grown up they are by helping out with chores at school, for example. Encourage this. You may even want to relate the skill to a discussion of community helpers and how they make our communities run more smoothly.

GROUPING OPTIONS
Whole group
Pairs

MATERIALS

- stack of books
- copies of page 62 (1 per child)
- crayons
- scissors
- tape
- blank paper

Teachable Moments

As you see children offering to help one another in the classroom, let them know you see their efforts to help their peers. Or provide a badge, such as the one made for Skill Lesson 2, that says "I Helped Out" or "I'm a Great Helper." Repeat a child's words when you overhear someone offering help; for example, "I heard Russell say 'I can help you reach that toy, Josh.' Thank you, Russell, for being helpful."

Introduce the Skill

1. Ask children to watch what you are doing as you try to lift a heavy stack of books. Say: *If you saw someone trying to lift a lot of books as I am doing, what might you do?* Have children tell about times they have helped another person. Then ask them how they felt when they helped. Point out that we feel happy, good, or proud when we can help someone else. Talk about why we need to help one another and what might happen if we didn't help out.

2. To model the skill, invite a child to pantomime trying to lift a heavy stack of books. Offer to help by asking, "Do you need help?" and then show how you might help out. Have children suggest other ways one might offer help, such as asking, "How can I help?" or "Would you like some help?" Brainstorm ways to help with the task, such as carrying a few books at a time, loading a wagon, or enlisting the help of others to create an "assembly line."

3. Try to give each child the opportunity to come up to you and ask if you need help. Vary the situations. For example, say, "I can't find my red pen" or "I have the entire chalkboard to erase."

Help Children Respond

1. Provide situations such as the ones below, then discuss with children ways they might help. Divide the group into pairs and have each pair pretend they are in one of the situations and act out what they would do.
   - A teacher is holding pencils that need sharpening.
   - A classmate is having trouble taking off her boots.
   - A classmate who is shorter than you is trying to reach something on a high shelf.
   - Everything is falling out of a friend's backpack.
   - A classmate is getting frustrated trying to tie his shoes.

2. Have children discuss how they help people. Then distribute copies of page 62. Help children fill in the blanks with their name and the name of someone they've helped. Ask them to color the building, cut it out, and cut out the door so that it opens. Then help them

paste the sides of the building onto a blank piece of paper. Where the door opens, they can draw themselves helping in some way. Tape the papers together to make a collaborative banner.

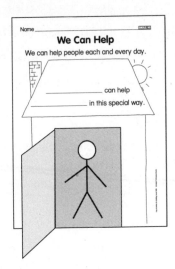

Book Break

Helping Out by George Ancona
(Houghton Mifflin, 1985)
The photographs in this book may inspire children to think of ways they can help those around them.

The Little Engine That Could by Watty Piper
(Grossett & Dunlap, 1978)
This classic story demonstrates how size and strength matter less than the willingless to help unselfishly.

Jamaica's Find by Juanita Havill
(Scholastic, 1986)
Finders keepers, losers weepers? When a little girl finds a stuffed animal, her empathy helps the owner get the dog back.

Try This, Too!

Title a class chart or corner of the chalkboard "Today's Helpers." Each day identify one or more children who initiate helping others and write their names on a list. You also may want to involve the class in a project to help in their community—cleaning a park, planting a neighborhood garden, collecting food for the homeless, or visiting senior citizens.

MATERIALS
- chart paper or chalkboard
- marker or chalk

Standing Up for Yourself

Children have the right to feel safe, to say no, and to voice some opinions or complaints. Understanding that they have these rights is important so that children can stand up for themselves and feel good about it. Help children understand that expressing themselves can empower them to improve a situation.

GROUPING OPTIONS
Whole group
Pairs

MATERIALS
- 2 puppets
- copies of page 63 (1 per child)
- crayons
- scrap materials (optional)
- scissors
- craft sticks
- paste or tape

Teachable Moments

Reinforce the moments when assertive behavior by children seems appropriate by remarking, "You did the right thing" or "Thank you for making your complaint without whining." Remind children that we are in charge of choosing what we do more often than we may think. So if we don't feel comfortable doing something, we can say so, explain why, and not do it.

Introduce the Skill

1. Ask children to sit in a circle. Ask: *Have you ever wanted to say no to something but didn't?* Encourage a lively discussion. Then introduce the puppets, one on each hand. Have children listen to the puppets' conversation:

   PUPPET 1: *Is that your CD?*

   PUPPET 2: *No, it's not.*

   PUPPET 1: *Let's go to the listening center and play it.*

   PUPPET 2: *It must belong to someone. If we take it to the listening center and the person who owns it comes back, she won't know what happened to it.*

   PUPPET 1: *You never want to have fun! Do you want to hear that CD or not?*

   PUPPET 2: *No, I'm sorry. I think that taking it is wrong and I won't do it.*

2. Discuss with children how Puppet 2 refused to do something. Ask: *How do you think she handled the situation?* Then improvise the puppet play several times with volunteers working Puppet 2 while a volunteer works Puppet 1. Offer helpful suggestions.

3. Next, work both puppets while children observe the following conversation:

   PUPPET 1: *Why weren't you in school last week, Polka Dot Face?*

   PUPPET 2: *Those spots are from chicken pox.*

   PUPPET 1: *Okay, Polka Dot Face.*

   PUPPET 2 (uses a strong voice): *My name is Charlotte!*

   PUPPET 1: *Charlotte Polka Dot Face!*

   PUPPET 2: *It hurts my feelings when I'm called names.*

   PUPPET 1: *But your name is Charlotte Polka Dot Face!*

   PUPPET 2: (walks away)

4. Mention that Puppet 2 was teasing Puppet 1 by calling her a silly name. Discuss ways to react to this kind of situation by asking children what Puppet 2 did. Explain that Puppet 2 looked right at Puppet 1, used a strong voice, and said "My name is ___." When Puppet 1 continued to tease, Puppet 2 walked away.

5. Point out that sometimes a person does something wrong to get attention. If we don't pay attention, then the person will most likely stop.

6. Explain to children that they have rights. First, they have the right to feel safe. When they feel unsafe, children should share these feelings with a grown-up they trust. Second, they have the right to say no—in a nice way—when they feel afraid or think something is wrong. Last, they have the right to give their opinion to make things better. It is important to speak up to let others know how we feel or how we want to be treated.

Help Children Respond

1. Distribute copies of page 63 and other materials so that children can create stick puppets of their own. After they color and decorate the puppet, help them cut along the dotted outline, and paste or tape a craft stick on back of the puppet.

2. Provide situations for pairs of children to use their puppets to act out the situations below.
   - Someone cuts in line for the water fountain.
   - One person won't share a box of crayons.
   - An older kid calls you a baby.
   - Someone tells you to hide a special toy that a classmate has brought for sharing.
   - Two classmates want you to help them knock down part of a child's block tower.

   After each puppet play, talk about the behavior and, if necessary, provide suggestions for how to correct behavior.

Try This, Too!

Mention to children that people who are friends try to be good to each other. Brainstorm with children a list of things friends don't do. Give a few examples to help them get started. For example: *Friends don't call each other names. Friends don't yell at each other. Friends don't say mean things.* Add each idea to a chart. Reread the completed chart and invite children to join in.

Friends don't . . .
- call each other names.
- yell at each other.
- say mean things.

----- **Book Break** -----

Chrysanthemum
by Kevin Henkes
(Greenwillow, 1991)
A girl who is teased about her unusual name learns how special it is.

Angel Child, Dragon Child
by Michele Maria Surat
(Scholastic, 1989)
A boy who teases a new girl at school later initiates a community effort to enable her Vietnamese mother to join the family in the United States.

How to Be a Friend: A Guide to Making Friends and Keeping Them **by Laurie Krasny Brown and Marc Brown**
(Little, Brown, 1998)
This child-friendly book addresses the ups and downs of friendship, including how to deal with bossy friends and bullies.

MATERIALS
- chart paper or poster board
- markers

Dealing With Anger

Children need to be aware that everyone gets angry and that it's okay to feel that way and to express their anger. They need to learn alternatives to physical action and aggressive words as ways to express anger. Help children develop appropriate ways of dealing with and controlling anger. Pausing a moment between an impulse and an action is an important skill.

GROUPING OPTIONS
Whole group

MATERIALS
- chart paper or poster board
- marker
- copies of page 64 (1 per child)

Teachable Moments

Support children who control their anger and walk away from a situation or use alternate strategies rather than becoming angered in the classroom. Distribute badges from Skill Lesson 2 that say, "Cool as a cucumber."

Introduce the Skill

1. Read children the following story:

   One day at school, a boy was building with blocks. A girl came by and asked to use the blocks. When the boy didn't answer, the girl grabbed some blocks. The boy tried to cover them up with his body. Then the girl kicked the building he was making. The boy started to yell loudly, calling her a name. Soon, the teacher had to close the block corner so the two children could talk about their problem.

2. Allow time for the children to think about the story. Then ask: *What went wrong? Why? How do you know the girl was angry?* (She grabbed and kicked.) *What could she have done instead?* (She could have asked again, politely.) *How do you know the boy was angry?* (He yelled.) *What could he have said instead?* (He could have said, "I'm angry that my building was kicked.") Ask: *If you are angry with another person, does grabbing, kicking, or pushing make the problem better or worse?* You might mention that "getting back" never makes a problem better and often makes it worse!

3. Encourage children to tell how they feel about an action rather than blaming the person who did the action. For example, when you play a game with someone who doesn't play by the rules, you might say, "I don't like it when you cheat," rather than saying, "You're a cheater!"

4. Now reread the story, adding some of the suggestions children made. For example:

   One day at school, a boy was building with blocks. A girl came by and asked to use the blocks. When the boy didn't answer, the girl grabbed some blocks. The boy tried to cover them up with his body. The girl felt like kicking the building the boy was making. But she knew to stop, think, and calm down before saying or doing anything. Then she said, "I'm angry because I didn't get an answer when I asked to use the blocks. Then I got angrier so I took some."

   The boy said, "I'm angry because the blocks I wanted to use were grabbed." Soon they came up with a plan. They divided up the remaining

blocks. She agreed not to touch the ones he was already building with. He agreed not to cover up the remaining blocks. And most important, they were still friends!

5. Ask children to talk about what happened this time. Help them identify that a child recognized her angry feelings; she stopped, thought, and calmed down before saying and doing anything; each child told what was done to make him or her angry and agreed not to do it again. Point out that if the boy and girl in the story couldn't have agreed, then they might have asked an adult for help. It is important for children to understand that expressing their feelings is fine, but it needs to be done in a way that doesn't hurt others.

Help Children Respond

1. Explain that when we are angry, we may need to calm down before we do something about it. Practice relaxation techniques with children, such as closing your eyes and counting to 10 silently; or breathing deeply through the nose and releasing the breath slowly through the mouth. Encourage children, when they are angry, to do this a few times until they feel calmer.

2. Ask children to think of other things that they can do when they feel angry. Record their responses on chart paper in a numbered list titled "What I Can Do if I'm Angry."

3. Distribute copies of page 64 to children and talk together about what is happening in each illustration:
   A. Someone grabs a book another child is reading.
   B. Someone pushes someone else on the playground.
   C. Someone is very noisy while another child is trying to listen at a listening center.
   D. An adult is angry at children who are running in the hall.

   Ask children to think about the strategies on the chart you've just made. Discuss which of the strategies they think might work for each situation.

Try This, Too!

Make a collaborative journal for children to help them control their anger. Help children fold their paper in half. Ask children to draw pictures of a situation when they became angry on the left and how they handled the situation on the right. Combine the pictures for a class journal of strategies that work.

Book Break

The Grouchy Ladybug
by Eric Carle
(HarperCollins, 1996)
In this circular story, a ladybug who forgets her manners and doesn't choose to share picks fights with creatures bigger than herself.

***When Sophie Gets Angry—
Really, Really Angry***
by Molly Bang
(Scholastic, 1999)
This Caldecott Honor book describes how a little girl deals with anger by removing herself from the situation to appreciate the calming effect of nature.

What I Can Do if I'm Angry

1. Count to 10 silently.
2. Take a few deep breaths.
3. Walk away.
4. Tell the person I am angry.
5. Tell a grown-up how I feel.
6. Draw a picture that shows how I feel.

MATERIALS
- 8½-inch by 11-inch drawing paper (1 per child)
- crayons
- stapler

Using Voice and Body Control

Help children develop self-control of their bodies. Some children need to practice self-control by keeping their hands to themselves. Other children need to learn to use a moderate voice level in the classroom.

GROUPING OPTIONS

Whole group
Small groups
Pairs

MATERIALS

- puppet
- paper lunch bags
- markers
- scrap materials such as yarn, cloth materials, pipe cleaners, and so on
- paste

Teachable Moments

Notice and mention when children use a moderate tone of voice and appropriate body control. Be a good role model by using an appropriate tone of voice at all times and thinking before you speak, no matter how you feel.

Introduce the Skill

1. Have children sit in a circle on chairs. Hold a puppet and go around the circle to various children, speaking in a loud voice for the puppet. You might say things such as, "Hello," "My name is ___," or "How are you today?" You might also put the puppet's face very close to the child to whom you are speaking.

2. Ask children how they felt about the puppet's voice. Was it too loud? Was it uncomfortable to listen to? Was it annoying when the puppet was so close?

3. Talk about the appropriate volume to use in the classroom, pointing out that working and playing together can make for a very noisy space, especially indoors. Model how to use an "inside voice" that is loud enough to hear but that doesn't hurt your ears. Have children practice saying a sentence using an inside voice. Tell children that the puppet will come and speak to each and every one of them. Ask them to determine whether the puppet is using an inside/soft voice or an outside/loud voice.

4. Many young children tend to touch peers when speaking. Remind children that some people don't like to be touched, that in order for their words to be heard they may want to keep their hands "quiet."

5. Discuss physical ways we might deal with our feelings. For example, if we are proud of a friend, we might pat the friend on the back, offer a hug, or give a high-five. If we are angry, however, it is never okay to hit.

Help Children Respond

1. Sit with children in the circle, holding a puppet. Go around the circle and ask each child to respond to the puppet's question, for example: *When is your birthday? What is your favorite toy (food, book)?* Reinforce each response by saying, "I like the inside voice you used. I can hear you and it doesn't hurt my ears," or "Shhh! Your outside voice is hurting my ears."

2. Have children work with puppets to practice using their inside voices. Help them make paper bag puppets. Here's how: Keep a paper lunch bag folded, with the rectangular bottom facing front and the open end facing down. Children can create a face on the bag's rectangular bottom using scrap materials, yarn, pipe cleaners, markers, and other odds and ends. They can decorate the front of the bag as the puppet's body. After the paste dries, show children how to put their hand inside to open and close the puppet's mouth.

3. Later, provide practice with appropriate body control. Invite a volunteer to help you demonstrate actions, such as shaking hands and gently patting on the back or arm. Have children practice with partners. After each pair demonstrates, praise appropriate actions.

Book Break

Noisy Nora by Rosemary Wells (Penguin, 2000)
A middle child continually makes noise, much to her family's dismay.

Try This, Too!

At different times during the school day, give one child the job of listening for outside voices in the classroom. The monitor can approach a peer who is speaking too loudly and whisper to him or her—a quiet way to remind the person to use an "inside voice."

Accepting Consequences

Consequential thinking is an emerging skill for four- and five-year-olds.
When children recognize that their words and actions have consequences,
then they are better able to take responsibility.

GROUPING OPTIONS
Whole group
Individuals

MATERIALS
■ copies of page 65
■ crayons
■ stapler

Introduce the Skill

1. Tell children: *Today we're going to listen to a story about a bunny and decide how it ends.* Read the following story:

   Becky Bunny has been chomping on carrots that were on the kitchen table. Her mother hops in and warns Becky she will have no dinner if the carrots needed for the stew are eaten. Her mother leaves the room, and Becky forgets her mom's warning. She continues to eat the carrots. When it's time to make the stew, her mother is upset that no carrots are left. "Did you eat the rest of the carrots?" Mother asks.

   Becky looks up and says:

   a. "Gee, Mom, I have no idea what happened to them."
   b. "Oops! Gotta run! I'm late for my bunny hop class!"
   c. "I did. I'm sorry. I was so hungry, I forgot to save some for the stew."

   Discuss each choice with the group. Have children vote on what Becky Bunny should say. Point out that by admitting that she ate the carrots and saying, "I'm sorry," Becky is taking responsibility for her actions. If we do something wrong, then we must be willing to accept the consequences. Ask what the consequence of Becky Bunny eating all the carrots is. (no dinner)

2. Remind children that a consequence is what happens after we do something. Give a few examples:
   • You drink hot chocolate that is too hot. What happens next?
   • Your library book is overdue. What happens next?
   • You oversleep one Monday morning. What might be a consequence?

   You may want to mention some class rules and have children identify consequences for following/not following them.

Teachable Moments

When children make mistakes or use inappropriate behavior in the classroom but accept the consequences of their actions without complaining, acknowledge their efforts. Point out how saying you are sorry and/or doing something about it can prevent disagreements from getting worse—and often stops another person from continuing an argument.

Help Children Respond

Hand out copies of page 65. Discuss the picture with children. Point to the child who is not helping with the baking, to what she touched and shouldn't have; and to the child offering help. Then, ask:

- How do you think the other children might feel?

- If the children wanted to bake, what do you think they had to do first? (wash their hands)

- What might the girl think after she touches the dough with dirty hands? (that she made a mistake)

- What might she say to the boy? ("I'm sorry.")

- How do you think the boy would feel if the girl apologized? (better)

- How do you think the boy would feel if the girl did not apologize? (angry)

- What else might the girl do? (wash her hands) Is that a good idea or not? Who has a different idea?

- What might the consequence be for not following the rule of washing hands before baking? (She would not be allowed to bake; she might spread germs with her dirty hands.)

Suggest that children offer different ideas to these last questions. Ask them to draw an idea on the bottom half of page 65 to show a possible consequence of the girl's behavior. Collect children's drawings and combine the pages to make a collaborative book.

Book Break

Lilly's Purple Plastic Purse
by Kevin Henkes
(Greenwillow, 1996)
When Lilly ignores her teacher's request, she is unhappy with the consequences and then regrets her actions.

The Little Red Hen
by Paul Galdone
(Houghton Mifflin, 1985)
When friends neglect helping the hen make a cake, they suffer the consequence—not eating it—and learn to help out in the future.

Try This, Too!

Distribute copies of page 66, and ask children to describe the problem pictured in the middle box. Ask: *How do you think the girl feels? How do you think the boy who knocked over the juice feels?* Help children cut out, fold, and tape the pictures on page 66 into a cube. Have them place the cubes in front of them with the "problem" picture facing up. Have them turn their cubes so that each of the five "solution" pictures are discussed—not evaluated, however. Then have children work in small groups to roll their cubes and decide whether or not each solution that appears faceup is a positive one. Be sure to comment on each child's assessment of the consequences of each solution as you travel from group to group.

MATERIALS
- copies of page 66
- scissors
- tape

Activity Masters
for Skill Lessons

This thumbprint belongs to

This thumbprint belongs to

_____

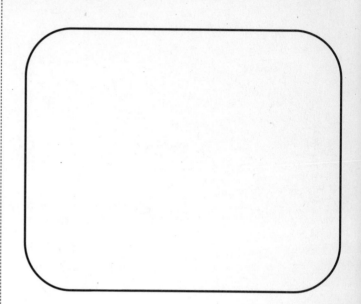

This thumbprint belongs to

_____

_____

SKILL 1

My Thumbprint Book

_____

by _____

This is my thumbprint.

Paper Doll
Template

I am special because

_____

_____

Easy Activities for Building Social Skills Scholastic Professional Books

Name _____

The Best Badge

Name _____

Name _____

Easy Activities for Building Social Skills Scholastic Professional Books

Don is silly.

8

My Feelings Book

Easy Activities for Building Social Skills   Scholastic Professional Books   page 49

by _____

I

Pam is afraid.

6

Maria is happy.

3

Ling is angry.

2

Easy Activities for Building Social Skills   Scholastic Professional Books page 50

Mako is excited.

7

Matt is surprised.

4

Zack is shy.

5

Name _____

Let's Play

If _____ ,

then _____

52

Name _____

What a Good Listener!

When I stop (STOP) ,

look 👀 ,

and listen 👂👂 ,

I learn that . . . .

_____

_____

We wave.

We smile.

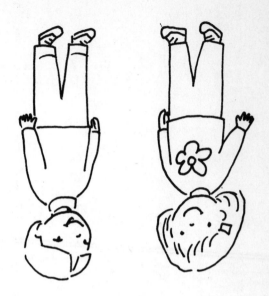

We both say, "Hi!"

SKILL 6

Hi!

by _____

Name _____

The Please and Thank You Game

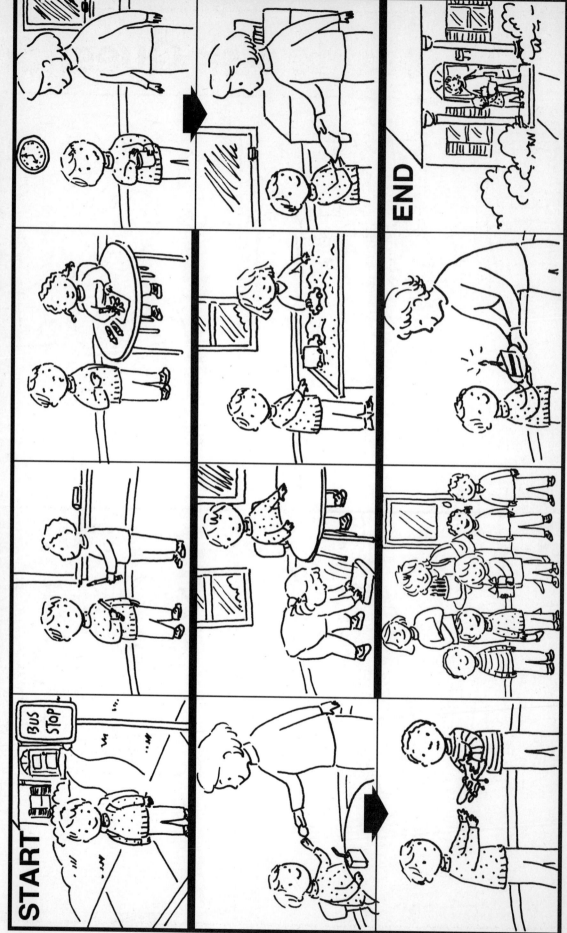

Easy Activities for Building Social Skills Scholastic Professional Books

It's Good to Ask Questions!

Name _____

Telephone Talk

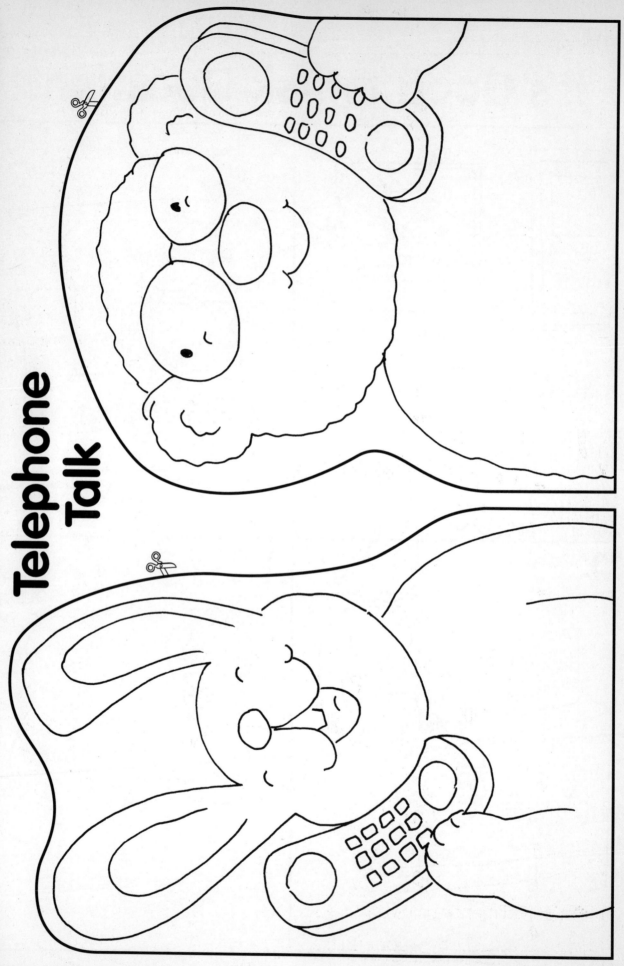

Easy Activities for Building Social Skills Scholastic Professional Books

The Compliment Tree

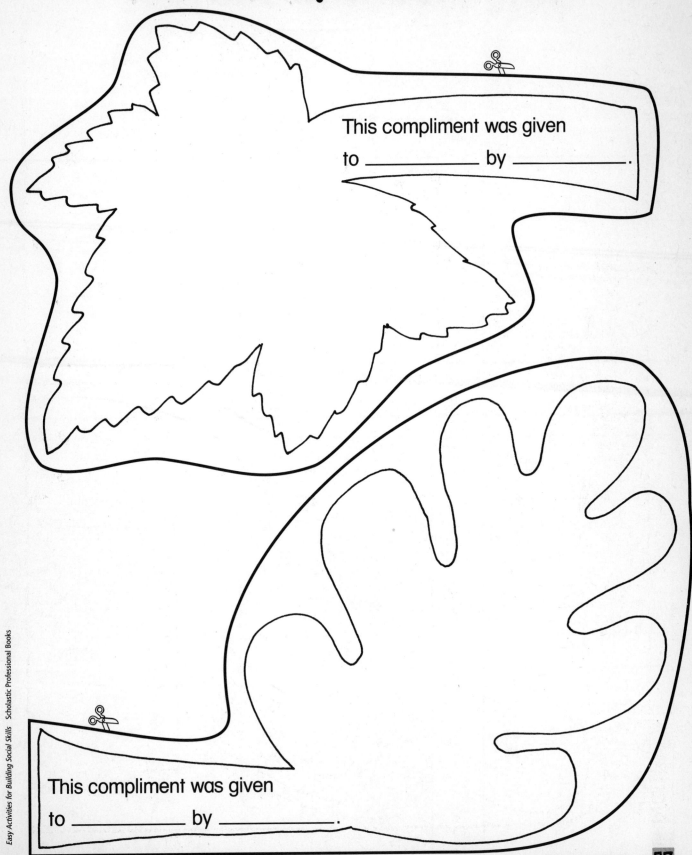

This compliment was given

to _____ by _____ .

This compliment was given

to _____ by _____ .

I Want to Play

1

2

3

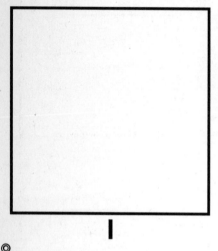

Can I play?

or

or

or

FOLD

FOLD

What Would You Do?

Make a Partner Puzzle

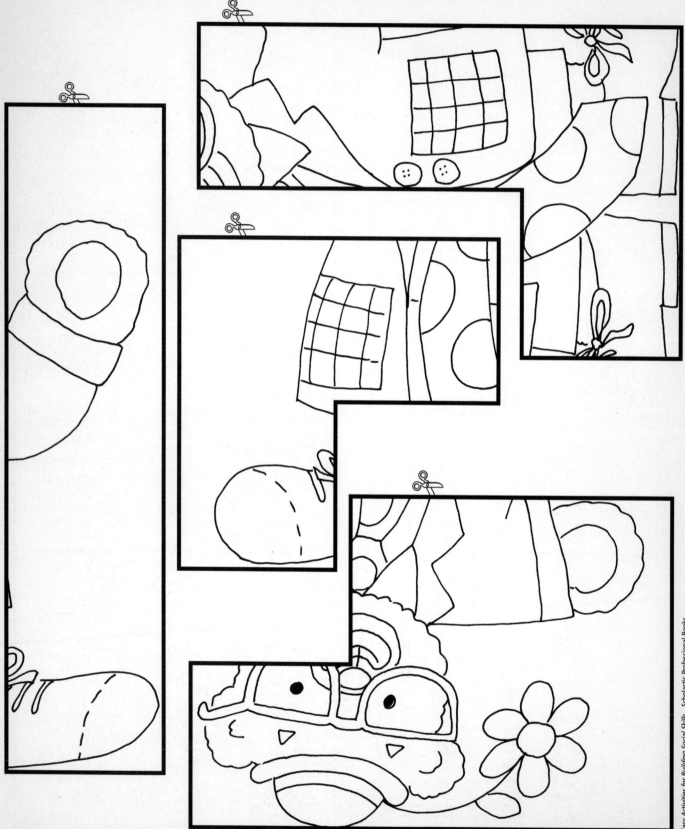

Easy Activities for Building Social Skills   Scholastic Professional Books

Name _____

Five Little People

Five little people played a game at school.   [Hold up 5 fingers.]

The first one said, "We follow each rule."   [Wiggle thumb.]

The second one said, "We help others learn."   [Wiggle next finger.]

The third one said, "We wait for our turn."   [Wiggle middle finger.]

The fourth one said, "We talk nicely and care."   [Wiggle next finger.]

The fifth one said, "We always play fair."   [Wiggle little finger.]

Five little people had fun that day!   [Hold up 5 separated fingers.]

They learned fair play is the only way!

61

We Can Help

We can help people each and every day.

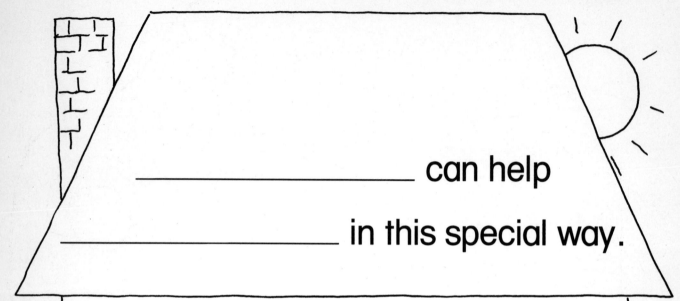

_____ can help

_____ in this special way.

Open the door
to see.

Easy Activities for Building Social Skills   Scholastic Professional Books

Stand Up and Be Counted

What I Can Do If I'm Angry

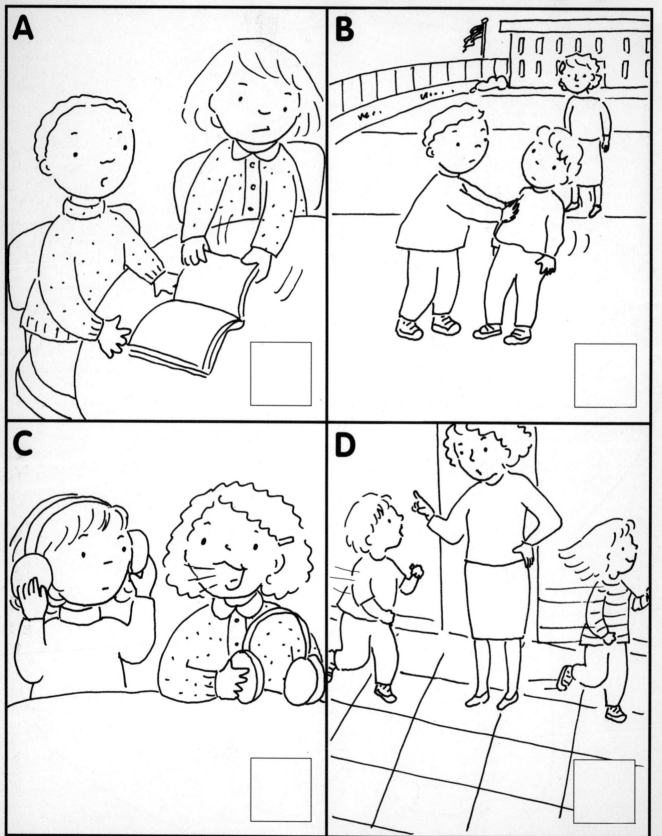

What Might Happen?

Let's Solve This Problem!

Name _____

Easy Activities for Building Social Skills Scholastic Professional Books

Teacher Resources

How to Communicate: Be Positive!

There are lots of ways to let children know they are doing good work in school. Here are a few alternatives to saying, "Good!" or to communicating, "Good work!" nonverbally. Also acknowledge what specific behavior was positive and why.

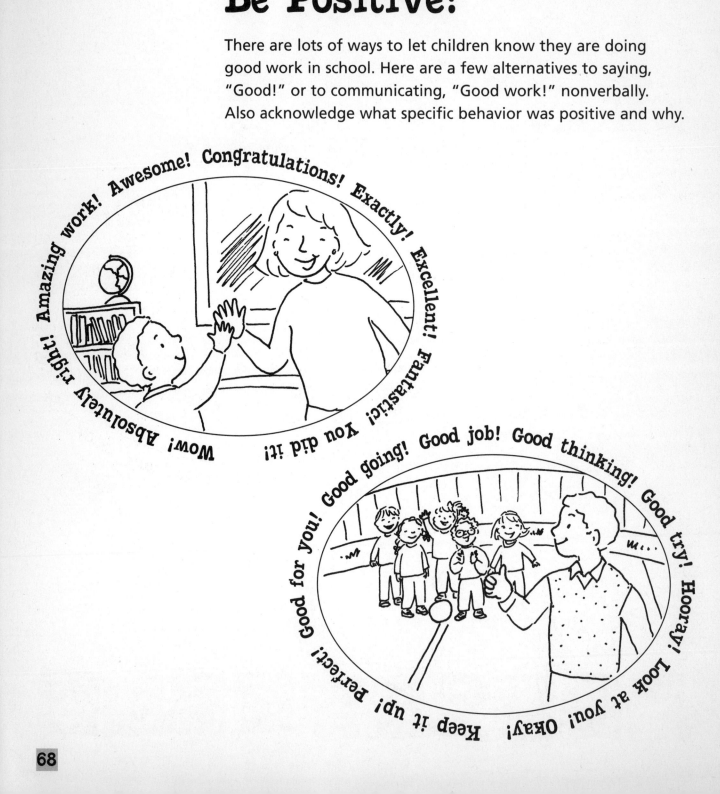

Amazing work! Awesome! Congratulations! Exactly! Excellent! Fantastic! You did it! Wow! Absolutely right!

Good for you! Good going! Good job! Good thinking! Good try! Hooray! Look at you! Okay! Keep it up! Perfect!

I love it! How wonderful! You deserve a pat on the back! Nice work! Right! Terrific job! I knew you could do it!

You should be so proud of yourself! That's it! Way to go! Well done! You got it! That's great! You remembered!

What an idea! Super-duper! You learn quickly! You thought of that by yourself! That's right! That's the way!

Checklist for Self-Evaluation

Directions: Make copies of page 71 and use it to help children self-assess their own developing social skills. Ask the child to put his or her finger on the shape of the row you mention. Once you see that he or she is in the correct place, ask the child to listen carefully as you read the statement. Tell the child to color in the picture that describes how he or she feels—the happy face to agree with what you said; the sad face to disagree with what you said, or the question mark if the child is not sure how he or she feels. Note: The **boldface titles** reference each skill lesson.

Accepting Differences in Others
Number 1: You like people for whoever they are, even if they are different from you.

Recognizing Strengths
Number 2: You are good at certain things.

Recognizing Nonverbal Language
Number 3: You can tell how someone is feeling by the person's face or actions.

Recognizing the Feelings of Others
Number 4: You can recognize when people are happy or sad from what they say and do.

Listening
Number 5: It is easy to listen and understand what someone says to you.

Greeting
Number 6: You say hello or smile when you see someone you know.

Using Polite Words
Number 7: You use kind words like "please" and "thank you."

Asking Questions
Number 8: You ask someone when you are not sure about what to do.

Using the Telephone
Number 9: You speak politely on the telephone.

Encouraging
Number 10: You say something nice to someone who has done a job well or who tries hard.

Joining In
Number 11: It is easy for you to join a group if you want to play.

Waiting Your Turn
Number 12: You wait your turn when you play or need someone's help.

Taking Turns/Sharing
Number 13: You take turns when you play and share your things with friends.

Being a Good Sport
Number 14: You play by the rules and are a good sport whether you win or lose.

Helping Others
Number 15: You ask for help if you need it.

Standing Up for Yourself
Number 16: You don't get too upset if someone bothers you or teases you.

Dealing With Anger
Number 17: You stay calm when you are angry.

Using Voice and Body Control
Number 18: You use an inside voice when you are indoors and you keep your hands to yourself.

Accepting Consequences
Number 19: You understand that when you have done something wrong, you are responsible for your actions.

Name

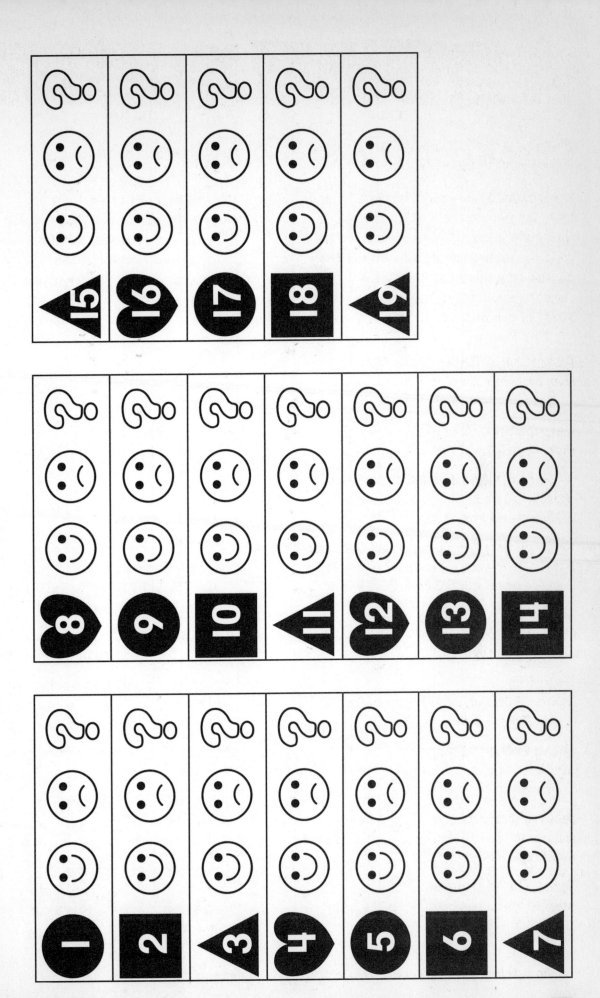

Teacher Checklist for Individual Skills Evaluation

Date _____

Child's Name _____ Date of Birth _____

SKILL	ALWAYS	OFTEN	SOMETIMES	SELDOM	NEVER	COMMENTS
1. Accepting Differences in Others						
2. Recognizing Strengths						
3. Recognizing Nonverbal Language						
4. Recognizing the Feelings of Others						
5. Listening						
6. Greeting						
7. Using Polite Words						
8. Asking Questions						
9. Using the Telephone						
10. Encouraging						
11. Joining In						
12. Waiting Your Turn						
13. Taking Turns/Sharing						
14. Being a Good Sport						
15. Helping Others						
16. Standing Up for Yourself						
17. Dealing With Anger						
18. Using Voice and Body Control						
19. Accepting Consequences						

Easy Activities for Building Social Skills   Scholastic Professional Books

Date _____

Teacher Checklist for Group Skills Evaluation

Directions: Put a check mark in a column when a skill has been demonstrated.

STUDENTS' NAMES

SKILL																
1. Accepting Differences in Others																
2. Recognizing Strengths																
3. Recognizing Nonverbal Language																
4. Recognizing the Feelings of Others																
5. Listening																
6. Greeting																
7. Using Polite Words																
8. Asking Questions																
9. Using the Telephone																
10. Encouraging																
11. Joining In																
12. Waiting Your Turn																
13. Taking Turns/Sharing																
14. Being a Good Sport																
15. Helping Others																
16. Standing Up for Yourself																
17. Dealing With Anger																
18. Using Voice and Body Control																
19. Accepting Consequences																

Books to Read

Books for Children

Ancona, George. *Helping Out*. New York: Houghton Mifflin, 1985. **SKILL 15**

Aliki. *Manners*. New York: Greenwillow, 1990. **SKILLS 7, 9**

Aliki. *Feelings*. New York: Greenwillow, 1984. **SKILL 10**

Aliki. *The Many Lives of Benjamin Franklin*. New York: Simon & Schuster, 1988. **SKILL 2**

Bang, Molly. *When Sophie Gets Angry—Really, Really Angry*. New York: Scholastic, 1999. **SKILL 17**

Berenstain, Stan, and Jan Berenstain. *Berenstain Bears Get in a Fight*. New York: Random House, 1987.

Brown, Laurie Krasny, and Marc Brown. *How to Be a Friend: A Guide to Making Friends and Keeping Them*. Boston: Little, Brown, 1998. **SKILLS 5, 11, 16**

Brown, Tricia. *Someone Special Just Like You*. New York: Scholastic, 1984. **SKILL 1**

Buehner, Caralyn. *I Did It, I'm Sorry*. New York: Scholastic, 1998.

Carle, Eric. *The Grouchy Ladybug*. New York: HarperCollins, 1996. **SKILL 17**

Carlson, Nancy. *I Like Me!* New York: Penguin Books, 1990. **SKILL 1**

Chardiet, Bernice, and Grace Maccarone. *The Best Teacher in the World*. New York: Scholastic, 1990. **SKILL 8**

Cheltenham Elementary School Kindergartners. *We Are All Alike . . . We Are All Different*. New York: Scholastic, 1998. (Also a big book and teaching guide)

Crary, Elizabeth. *I'm Mad*. Seattle: Parenting Press, 1992. (Dealing With Feelings series)

Crary, Elizabeth. *I Want It*. Seattle: Parenting Press, 1996. (Children's Problem Solving Book)

Curtis, Jamie Lee. *Today I Feel Silly and Other Moods That Make My Day*. New York: HarperCollins, 1998. **SKILL 4**

Evans, Lezlie. *Sometimes I Feel Like a Storm Cloud*. Greenvale, NY: Mondo Publishing, 1999. **SKILL 4**

Freyman, Saxton, and Joost Elffers. *How Are You Peeling? Foods With Moods*. New York: Scholastic, 1999. **SKILL 3**

Gaeddert, LouAnn. *Noisy Nancy Norris*. New York: Doubleday, 1971.

Galdone, Paul. *The Little Red Hen*. Boston: Houghton Mifflin, 1985. **SKILL 19**

Giff, Patricia Reilly. *Ronald Morgan Goes to Bat*. New York: Penguin, 1990. **SKILLS 10, 14**

Havill, Juanita. *Jamaica's Find*. New York: Scholastic, 1986. **SKILL 15**

Henkes, Kevin. *Chrysanthemum*. New York: Greenwillow, 1991. **SKILL 16**

Henkes, Kevin. *Jessica*. William Morrow, 1998.

Henkes, Kevin. *Lilly's Purple Plastic Purse*. New York: Greenwillow, 1996. **SKILL 19**

Howard, Arthur. *Cosmo Zooms*. San Diego: Harcourt Brace, 1999. **SKILL 2**

Howe, James. *Horace and Boris But Mostly Dolores*. New York: Atheneum, 1999. **SKILL 11**

Hutchins, Pat. *The Doorbell Rang*. New York: HarperCollins, 1986. **SKILL 13**

Lachner, Dorothea. *Andrew's Angry Words*. New York: North-South Books, 1995.

Lalli, Judy. *I Like Being Me: Poems for Children About Feeling Special, Appreciating Others, and Getting Along*. Minneapolis: Free Spirit Publishing, 1997.

Lionni, Leo. *It's Mine!* New York: Alfred A. Knopf, 1985.

Lionni, Leo. *Swimmy*. New York: Alfred A. Knopf, 1963.

Maccarone, Grace. *I Have a Cold*. New York: Scholastic, 1999. **SKILL 7**

McGrath, Bob. *Oops! Excuse Me Please! and Other Mannerly Tales*. Hauppauge, NY: Barrons, 1998. **SKILLS 6, 9, 13, 14**

Modesitt, Jeanne. *Sometimes I Feel Like a Mouse*. New York: Scholastic, 1996. **SKILL 4**

Payne, Emmy. *Katy No-Pocket*. Boston: Houghton Mifflin, 1973.

Payne, Lauren Murphy, and Claudia Rohling. *We Can Get Along*. Minneapolis: Free Spirit Publishing, 1997.

Petty, Kate. *Feeling Left Out*. New York: Barrons, 1991. **SKILL 11**

Piper, Watty. *The Little Engine That Could*. New York: Grossett & Dunlap, 1978. **SKILL 15**

Prestine, Joan Singleton. *It's Hard to Share My Teacher*. Torrance, CA: Fearon, 1994. **SKILL 12**

Prestine, Joan Singleton. *Sometimes I Feel Awful*. Torrance, CA: Fearon, 1993.

Ross, Anna. *Say the Magic Word, Please*. New York: Random House, 1990. **SKILLS 6, 7**

Sendak, Maurice. *Where the Wild Things Are*. New York: HarperCollins, 1963.

Sparks, Michael. *My Very First Book of Manners*. Eugene, OR: Harvest House, 2000.

Spelman, Cornelia Maude. *When I Feel Angry*. Morton Grove, IL: Albert Whitman, 2000.

Steig, William. *Pete's a Pizza*. New York: HarperCollins, 1998.

Stephens, Helen. *What About Me?* New York: Dorling Kindersley, 1999.

Sturges, Philemon. *The Little Red Hen Makes a Pizza*. New York: Penguin, 1999.

Surat, Michele Maria. *Angel Child, Dragon Child*. New York: Scholastic, 1989. **SKILL 16**

Weller, Stella. *Yoga for Children*. San Francisco: Thorsons, 1996.

Wells, Rosemary. *Noisy Nora*. New York: Penguin, 2000. **SKILL 18**

Books for Parents

Beekman, S., and J. Homes. *Battles, Hassles, Tantrums and Tears: Strategies for Coping with Conflict and Making Peace at Home*. New York: Hearst Books, 1997.

Bullard, Sara. *Teaching Tolerance: Raising Open-Minded, Empathetic Children*. New York: Doubleday, 1993.

Clark, Lynn. *SOS! Help for Parents*. Bowling Green, KY: Parents Press, 1996.

Colorosa, Barbara. *Kids Are Worth It*. New York: Avon Books, 1995.

Crary, Elizabeth. *Kids Can Cooperate: A Practical Guide to Teaching Problem Solving*. Seattle: Parenting Press, 1984.

Curwin, Richard L., and Allen N. Mendler. *Am I in Trouble? Using Discipline to Teach Young Children Responsibility*. Santa Cruz, CA: ETR, 1991.

Dinkmeyer, Don, and Gary D. McKay. *The Parent's Handbook: Systematic Training for Effective Parenting.* New York: Random House, 1997.

Duke, Marshall P., Elisabeth A. Martin, and Stephen Nowicki, Jr. *Teaching Your Child the Language of Success.* Atlanta: Peachtree Publishers, 1996.

Eastman, M., and S. C. Rozen. *Taming the Dragon in Your Child: Solutions for Breaking the Cycle of Family Anger.* New York: John Wiley, 1994.

Faber, Adele, and Elaine Mazlish. *How to Talk So Kids Will Listen and Listen So Kids Will Talk.* New York: Avon Books, 1999.

Fisher, Gary, and Rhoda Cummings. *When Your Child Has LD (Learning Differences): A Survival Guide for Parents.* Minneapolis: Free Spirit Publishing, 1995.

Garbarino, James. *Raising Children in a Socially Toxic Environment.* San Francisco: Jossey-Bass, 1995.

Glenn, H. Stephen, and Jane Nelsen. *Raising Self-Reliant Children in a Self-Indulgent World: Seven Building Blocks for Developing Capable Young People.* Rocklin, CA: Prima Publishing, 1988.

Lowe, Paula C. *Care Pooling: How to Get the Help You Need to Care for the Ones You Love.* San Francisco: Berrett-Koehler, 1993.

Nelsen, Jane, H., Stephen Glenn, and Lynn Lott. *Positive Discipline A–Z: From Toddlers to Teens, 1001 Solutions to Everyday Parenting Problems.* Rocklin, CA: Prima Publishing, 1999.

Saunders, Carol Silverman. *Safe at School: Awareness and Action for Parents of Kids Grades K–12.* Minneapolis: Free Spirit Publishing, 1994.

Shafir, Rebecca Z. *The Zen of Listening: Mindful Communication in the Age of Distraction.* Wheaton, IL: Quest Books, 2000.

Shure, Myrna. *Raising a Thinking Child: Help Your Young Child to Resolve Everyday Conflicts and Get Along with Others.* New York: Pocket Books, 1996. (also audiocassette and workbook)

Strickland, Eric. "Let's Play Outside," *Parent and Child.* 8, no. 5 (April/May 2001): 60–65.

Turecki, Stanley. *The Difficult Child.* New York: Bantam Books, 1989.

Unell, Barbara C., and Jerry L. Wykoff. *20 Teachable Virtues: Practical Ways to Pass on Lessons of Virtues and Character to Your Children.* New York: Berkley, 1995.

Webster-Stratton, Carolyn et al. *The Incredible Years: A Trouble-Shooting Guide for Parents of Children Aged 3–8.* Kent, WA: Pacific Pipeline, 1992.

Zimbardo, Philip C., and Shirley Radl. *The Shy Child.* Garden City, NY: Doubleday, 1982.

Books for Teachers

Armstrong, Thomas. *Multiple Intelligences in the Classroom.* Alexandria, VA: Association for Supervision and Curriculum Development, 1994.

Ballare, Antonio, and Angelique Lampros. *Behavior Smart! Ready-to-Use Activities for Building Personal and Social Skills for Grades K–4.* West Nyack, NY: The Center for Applied Research in Education, 1994.

Beane, Allan L. *Bully Free Classroom: Over 100 Tips and Strategies for Teachers K–8.* Minneapolis: Free Spirit Publishing, 1999.

Begun, Ruth Weltman. *Social Skills Lessons and Activities. (PreK–Kindergarten, Grades 1–3)* West Nyack, NY: Society for the Prevention of Violence Against Children with the Center for Applied Research in Education, 1995.

Berman, Sheldon. *Children's Social Consciousness and the Development of Social Responsibility.* Albany: State University of New York Press, 1997.

Borba, Michele, and Craig Borba. *Self-Esteem: A Classroom Affair.* Vol. 2. Nashville, TN: School-Age Notes, 1985.

Cartledge, Gwendolyn, and JoAnne Fellows Milburn. *Teaching Social Skills to Children.* New York: Pergamon, 1986.

Charney, Ruth Sidney. *Teaching Children to Care: Management in the Responsive Classroom.* Greenfield, MA: Northeast Foundation for Children, 1991.

Cummings, Rhoda, and Gary Fisher. *The School Survival Guide for Kids with LD (Learning Differences).* Minneapolis: Free Spirit Publishing, 1991. (also audiocasette)

Freeman, Sabrina, and Lorelei Dake. *Teach Me Language.* Lynden WA: SKF Books, 1996.

Glasser, William. *Reality Therapy in Action.* New York: HarperCollins, 2000.

Gardner, Howard. *Multiple Intelligences: The Theory in Practice.* New York: Basic Books, 1993.

Goleman, Daniel. *Emotional Intelligence: Why It Can Matter More Than IQ.* New York: Bantam Books, 1997. (also audiocassette)

Gray, Carol. *Original Social Stories.* Arlington, TX: Future Horizons, 1993.

Hughes, J. N. *Cognitive Behavior Therapy in the Schools.* New York: Pergamon, 1988.

King, Cheryl, and Daniel S. Kirschenbaum. *Helping Young Children Develop Social Skills: The Social Growth Program.* Pacific Grove, CA: Brooks/Cole, 1992.

Letts, Nancy. *Creating a Caring Classroom.* New York: Scholastic, 1997.

Mannix, Darlene. *Social Skills Activities for Special Children.* West Nyack, NY: Center for Applied Research in Education, 1991.

McGinnis, Ellen, and Arnold P. Goldstein. *Skillstreaming in Early Childhood: Teaching Prosocial Skills to the Preschool and Kindergarten Child.* Champaign, IL: Research Press, 1990. (also *Skillstreaming in Early Childhood Program Forms*)

Miller, Sarah, Janine Brodine, and Terri Miller, eds. *Safe by Design: Planning for Peaceful School Communities.* Seattle: Committee for Children, 1996.

Payne, Lauren Murphy, and Claudia Rohling. *A Leader's Guide to We Can Get Along.* Minneapolis: Free Spirit Publishing, 1997.

Perry, Bruce D. "Promoting Nonviolent Behavior in Children," *Early Childhood Today* 16, no. 1 (September 2001): 26–29.

Rice, Judith. *The Kindness Curriculum.* St. Paul, MN: Redleaf Press, 1995.

Rubin, Zick. *Children's Friendship.* Cambridge: Harvard University Press, 1980.

Schmidt, Fran, and Alice Friedman. *Peacemaking Skills for Little Kids.* Miami: Peace Education Foundation, 1997.

Shure, Myrna. *I Can Problem Solve: An Interpersonal Cognitive Problem-Solving Program. (Volumes for Preschool and Kindergarten/ Primary Grades).* Champaign, IL: Research Press, 1992.

Smith, Charles. *The Peaceful Classroom: 162 Classroom Activities to Teach Preschoolers.* Beltsville, MD: Gryphon House, 1993.

Stephens, T. M. *Social Skills in the Classroom.* Columbus, OH: Cedar Press, 1978.

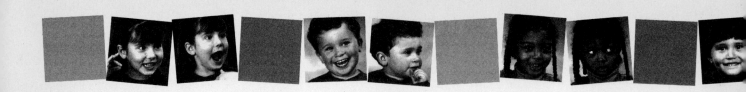

Teolis, Beth. *Ready-to-Use Conflict-Resolution Activities for Elementary Students*. West Nyack, NY: Center for Applied Research in Education, 1999.

Walker, Hill M., Geoff Colvin, and Elizabeth Ramsey. *Antisocial Behavior in School: Strategies and Best Practices.* San Francisco: Brooks/Cole, 1995.

Curricula

At Home in Our Schools: A Guide to School-Wide Activities that Build Community. Oakland, CA: Developmental Studies Center, 1997.

Heartwood Ethics Curriculum (PreK–4). New York: Scholastic.

Reading, Thinking, and Caring, Grades K–3. Oakland, CA: Developmental Studies Center, 1998.

Second Step (Pre/K). Seattle: Committee for Children, 1997.

Websites

www.autism.org/mnews

www.autism.org/social

www.cfchildren.org

www.earlychildhoodtoday.com

www.parentandchildonline.com

www.scholastic.com

www.uncg.edu/ericcass/violence

Videos

Churchill Media
12210 Nebraska Avenue
Los Angeles, CA 90025
(800) 334-7830
- *Courtesy? Who, Me?*
- *Feelings* series: *I'm Feeling Alone, I'm Feeling Happy, I'm Feeling Sad, I'm Feeling Scared, I'm Mad at Me, I'm Mad at You*
- *Solving Conflicts*
- *To Tell the Truth*
- *Values* series: *The Bike, The Hideout, Lost Puppy*

Coronet/MTI Film and Video
108 Wilmot Road
Deerfield, IL 60015
(800) 621-2131
- *Tell 'Em How You Feel*

Sunburst Communications
P.O. Box 40
Pleasantville, NY 10570-0040
(800) 431-1934
- *I'm So Frustrated!*
- *A Rainbow of Feelings*
- *No Fair!*
- *Everybody's Different*
- *Let's Be Friends*
- *We Can Work It Out!*
- *Stop Teasing Me!*
- *I Get So Mad!*

Notes

Notes